FENGSHUILOGY
SERIES

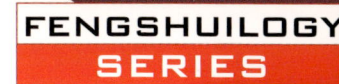

Your HEAD Here

by
Sherwin Ng

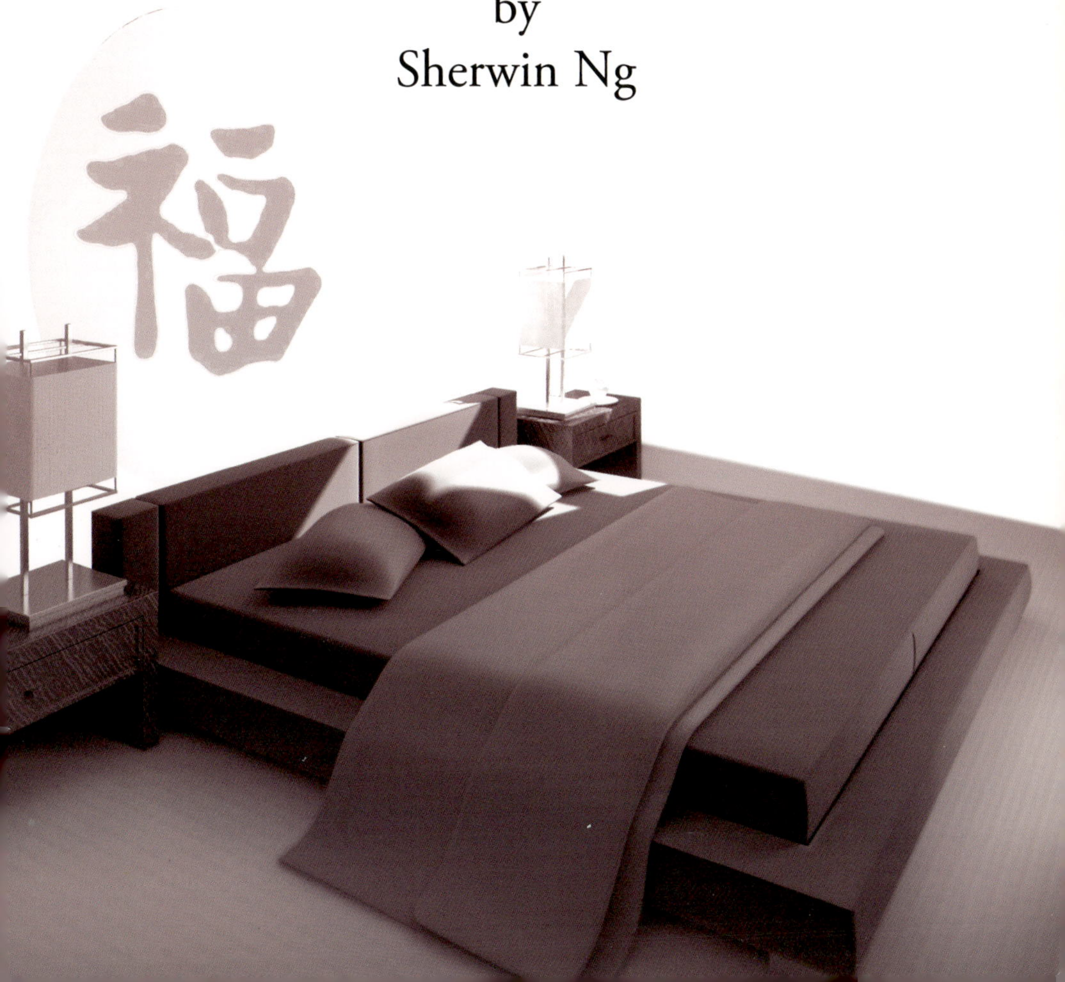

Your Head Here

Published in Kuala Lumpur, Malaysia by JY Books Sdn. Bhd. (659134-T)

Text © Sherwin Ng 2011
Design and illustrations © JY Books Sdn. Bhd.

First Edition July 2011

The author's moral rights have been asserted. All rights reserved worldwide. No part of this book may be copied, used, subsumed, or exploited in fact, field of thought or general idea, by any other authors or persons, or be stored in a retrieval system, transmitted or reproduced in any way, including but not limited to digital copying and printing in any form whatsoever worldwide without the prior agreement and written permission of the publisher.

Quantity discounts of JY Books titles are available for educational, business or sales promotional use. For information, please contact:

JY Books Sdn. Bhd. (659134-T)
19-3, The Boulevard, Mid Valley City, 59200 Kuala Lumpur, Malaysia.
Tel : +603-2284 8080 l Fax : +603-2284 1218 l Email : info@jy-books.com

DISCLAIMER:

The publisher JY Books Sdn Bhd and the author, Sherwin Ng, have made their best efforts to produce this high quality, informative and helpful book. They have verified the technical accuracy of the information and contents of this book. Any information pertaining to the events, occurrences, dates and other details relating to the person or persons, dead or alive, and to the companies have been verified to the best of their abilities based on information obtained or extracted from various websites, newspaper clippings and other public media. However, they make no representation or warranties of any kind with regard to the contents of this book and accept no liability of any kind for any losses or damages caused or alleged to be caused directly or indirectly from using the information contained herein.

Something shifted in the sky

a planet, a star, a fragment of

somebody's soul

shot across the night….

as when Hanuman ripped out

a piece of Himalaya

when no one was looking.

And something shifted…

— 'A Shift in the Sky',
Sherwin Ng

Dedicated to:

My father, Nick, for telling me wild stories of the immeasurable sky...

My mother, Julie, for showing me the roots that grow into the earth...

My sister, Trissha, my first best-friend, the isthmus to my estuary...

To all my teachers, past, present, and yet to come...

Acknowledgements:

This book would not have been possible without the following individuals:

Joey Yap, for opportunity, for lessons, for all your hard-work. Don't think I didn't notice, with my small eyes.

Jessie Lee, my colleague, for words of wisdom. Heartfelt appreciation, always and always.

Avi Ong, Cynthia Tan, and May Yoke Chan, for strategy, for time, and for beautiful artwork

Kenneth Cheng, Dave Tia, Teo Chang Ooi, my 3 Heroes who don't know they are heroes.

Yoganraj Ramadass, my very strong assistant, for keeping me moving and on track, for keeping the temperature cool always.

My 3 Graces in this lifetime: Ginnie Chua, Shiren Naidu, and Candy Moy – for constantly reminding me of my own brilliance, and never allowing me to apologize for it.

Table of Contents

Chapter 1:	An Introduction to Mountains and Feng Shui	1
Chapter 2:	Feng Shui Rules for the Bed	7
Chapter 3:	Mountainology	19
Chapter 4:	Using This Book	25
Chapter 5:	Homes Facing in Period 7	37
	Facing South 1 (丙)	38
	Facing South 2 (午) or South 3 (丁)	40
	Facing Southwest 1 (未)	42
	Facing Southwest 2 (坤) or Southwest 3 (申)	44
	Facing West 1 (庚)	46
	Facing West 2 (酉) or West 3 (辛)	48
	Facing Northwest 1 (戌)	50
	Facing Northwest 2 (乾) or Northwest 3 (亥)	52
	Facing North 1 (壬)	54
	Facing North 2 (子) or North 3 (癸)	56
	Facing Northeast 1 (丑)	58
	Facing Northeast 2 (艮) or Northeast 3 (寅)	60
	Facing East 1 (甲)	62
	Facing East 2 (卯) or East 3 (乙)	64
	Facing Southeast 1 (辰)	66
	Facing Southeast 2 (巽) or Southeast 3 (巳)	68
Chapter 6:	: Homes Facing in Period 8	71
	Facing South 1 (丙)	72
	Facing South 2 (午) or South 3 (丁)	74
	Facing Southwest 1 (未)	76
	Facing Southwest 2 (坤) or Southwest 3 (申)	78
	Facing West 1 (庚)	80
	Facing West 2 (酉) or West 3 (辛)	82
	Facing Northwest 1 (戌)	84
	Facing Northwest 2 (乾) or Northwest 3 (亥)	86
	Facing North 1 (壬)	88
	Facing North 2 (子) or North 3 (癸)	90
	Facing Northeast 1 (丑)	92
	Facing Northeast 2 (艮) or Northeast 3 (寅)	94
	Facing East 1 (甲)	96
	Facing East 2 (卯) or East 3 (乙)	98
	Facing Southeast 1 (辰)	100
	Facing Southeast 2 (巽) or Southeast 3 (巳)	102
Chapter 7:	Bedroom (Feng Shui) Secrets	105

Foreword by Joey Yap

When Sherwin Ng first joined my class he was one of my youngest students. Right off the bat, however, I saw potential in him that I have seldom seen in others since! Although Sherwin at first appeared shy and quiet, he showed a keen interest in Chinese metaphysics. He asked plenty of questions in his bid to get the most out of the classes he attended and it pretty soon became clear that he had a passion for the subject matter.

It is safe to say that Sherwin has been one of my most gifted students from Day 1. Sadly, he did not have the money necessary to continue his coursework once he had completed the first portion of it. I couldn't bear to lose him so I took him under my wing and decided to train him. With hindsight, this turned out of a great investment! As I got to know Sherwin I discovered that he is not at all shy and he is in fact very friendly and personable, going out of his way to be helpful. This made him perfect for a job on my consulting team. I invited him and he agreed.

In all the subsequent years that Sherwin has served as a consultant with me, I have received many compliments from clients commending Sherwin on his good work. These same clients have benefited from his consultations personally and financially. It became apparent that Sherwin was doing exceptional work and so I asked (forced, in the end!) him, using my capacity as a teacher and mentor, to try and share his knowledge with others. Having spent many years passing on my own expertise I knew how rewarding the experience could be. Sherwin had worked in a writing capacity for me in the past and so I knew that he may make a great author. Indeed, he had mentioned his desire to write a book of some kind in the past, but not necessarily one on Feng Shui.

When I first approached Sherwin to write the book about Feng Shui, he was hesitant. I would not be deterred however. He had proven during his time writing articles that he has a poetic flair for the written word. He certainly had the experience in Feng Shui to put together a book and I finally convinced him to do so in Germany on a trip to Frankfurt!

The book you are reading now is the first one that Sherwin has written. By his own admission, it took him longer than he expected to put it together but his hard work has paid off! The care he has put into this project is apparent to all because the book does an outstanding job of breaking down complex Feng Shui concepts into simple, concise instructions and advice that the layperson can understand. You don't need to have dedicated as much time to Feng Shui as Sherwin to make sense of this book and benefit from his wisdom! You can achieve a lot using this book and nothing else as it includes many handy techniques which generate quick results, all laid out for you in a straightforward "Feng Shui-It-Yourself" manner.

While it is true that there are many schools of thought and different systems when it comes to Feng Shui, this does not change the fundamental goal of Feng Shui: RESULTS. Whatever methods or techniques you use are useless unless they generate results and this book contains advice known to do just that for those willing to listen. As such, it has something to offer everyone interested in Feng Shui at any level!

The book itself focuses on Bedroom Feng Shui; specifically, how you should position your bed according to Classical Feng Shui in order to harness desirable effects for your health, personal life and career. Different people will benefit from different bed positions depending on what they are currently seeking in life; that is to say that what works for one person won't be good for another. The Bed is one of the Main Factors of Feng Shui, along with the Main Door and Stove and since you spend a lot of time in bed it is important that you put it in the right place!

Sherwin himself comes from a practical background – not just an academic one – and this means that the advice he gives herein is suitably practical.

I wish Sherwin all the best with this book and I am glad he finally came round to the idea of writing it! He can now reach more people than he could ever hope to through his consulting duties and so his passion for the subject can be spread further. Hope to see more books from him in the future!

Warmest regards,

Joey Yap
Founder of Mastery Academy of Chinese Metaphysics
July 2011

www.joeyyap.com
www.facebook.com/joeyyapFB

Preface

The idea of this book was conceived in a cab in Frankfurt late 2010, on the way to dinner and just after shopping at Hugo Boss. Joey said, "Why don't you write something interesting for the Fengshuilogy Series?"

It took me a long time to get this book done properly. I think while I accomplished this ONE, Joey has already written 10, since Frankfurt and now! But working on this project made me realized that while I may have not been conscious about it, I have been 'eating, sleeping, and living' Feng Shui for about 8 years of my life now, every single day. Along the way, I've managed to make many people happy, some richer (than me), and some just problem-less generally.

When I attended my first ever Feng Shui Module 1 and 2 over seven years ago, I never had the intention to become a Feng Shui consultant. I was on my way to becoming a clinical psychologist. But then as always, Destiny took a 93 degree turn and I soon had the opportunity to consult for Yap Global Consulting (now, Joey Yap Consulting Group). The learning curve was steep and I really had to bend backwards but forge ahead, especially in the first year. But I can say that until today, I still enjoy consulting and teaching Feng Shui very much. Sometimes you don't know you like it until you try it. And once you like it, you will naturally work harder on it.

Here's a sub-plot I do not often tell people: after my Feng Shui Module 1 & 2, I was fresh out of college, with not a penny to my name. So Joey gave me a job writing Feng Shui articles for the Academy. Of course, very soon I was able to afford Feng Shui Module 3 & 4 – and the rest, as you know now, is really history! But what I really want to tell you is that because of the Feng Shui knowledge I used for myself, my life has become, well, relatively easy – and so too, enjoyable.

So this book is a tribute to the Mastery Academy of Chinese Metaphysics, and its founder, Mr. Joey Yap. Not only for changing the lives of so many across the world, but mine as well.

All of the recommendations and formulas used in this book are what I personally would use for my own Feng Shui clients, and also myself. Much of the technicalities and some of the limitations of this book are addressed in Chapters 2 and 4.

Lastly, you might be wondering by now – why the title 'Your Head Here'? Firstly, it refers to the head of a bed (床頭), as well as the head of mountains (巒頭). I wanted it to be a fun book, like how the Chinese say, 'Your Head' （你的頭）, an unprofaned, but slightly irksome way of saying 'in your dreams', or 'not in a million years'.

Not in a million years I would have thought I would write a book on Feng Shui. For a long time I had dreamed it to be a collection of poetry, a romantically spiritual novel, or something else – but like I said, Destiny has its own twist on the way Life pans out. But all in good fun, and all in good faith. Who knows what we can achieve next, tomorrow?

Wishing you a delightful read.

Yours sincerely,

吳宸揚

Sherwin Ng
July 2011

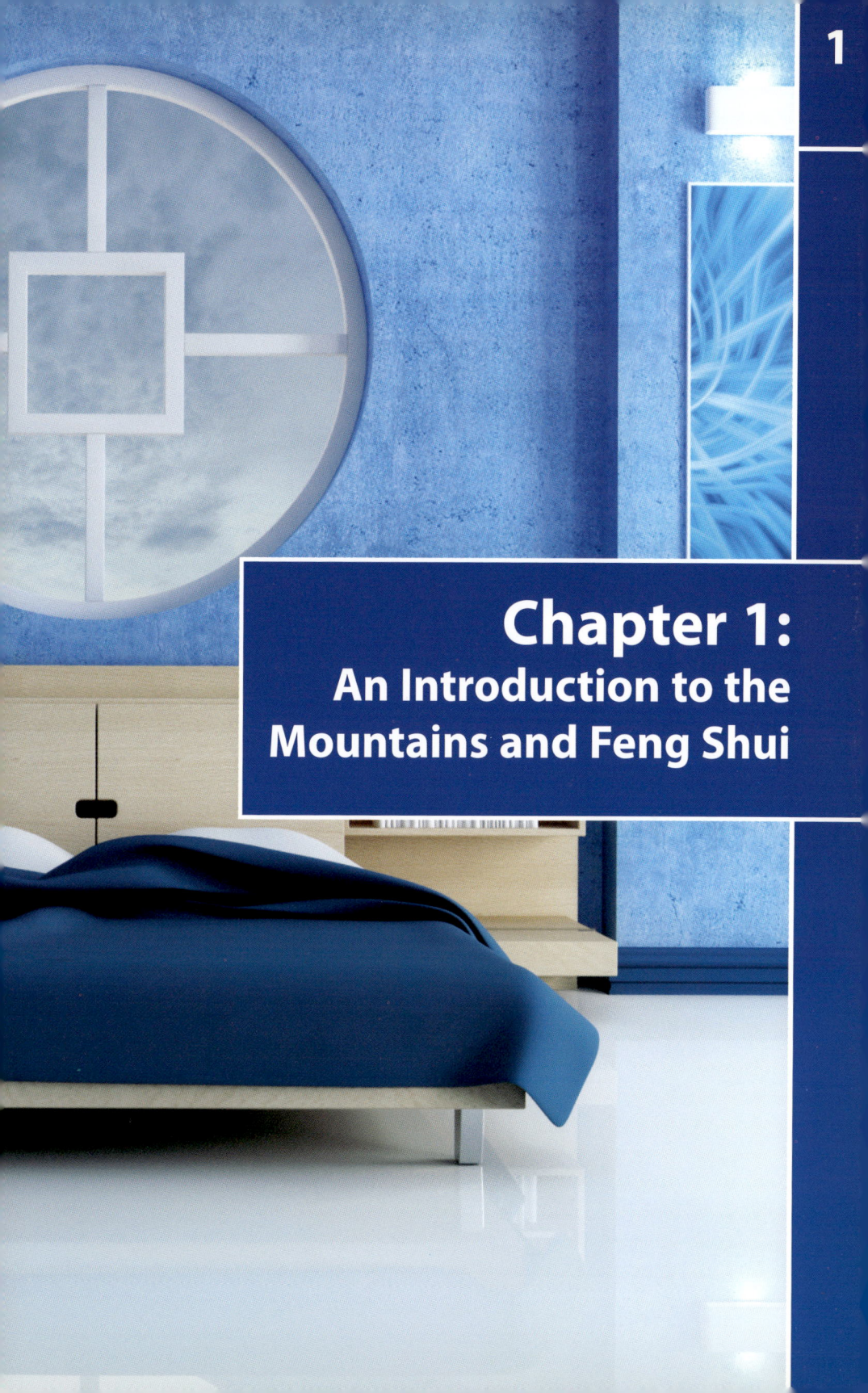

Chapter 1:
An Introduction to the Mountains and Feng Shui

An Introduction to the Mountains and Feng Shui

Since we already know Feng Shui means 'wind and water' – where do the mountains come into play? – where water is the active, Yang component of Nature, mountains are the stable, Yin component. Where water is the 'father', mountains are the 'mother' in Feng Shui. Yin meeting Yang or Yang meeting Yin is ultimate balance and Feng Shui harmony.

WATER	MOUNTAINS
Active = Yang	Stable = Yin

Role of Mountains in Feng Shui

乘風則散，界水則止
Qi is dispersed by the Wind and gathers at the boundaries of Water.

We have established that wind carries away Qi (and so very windy areas do not retain Qi well); we also know that water gathers Qi – so now the next thing you need to know is that mountains *produce* Qi. Mountains are the 'mothers' of the land, and they are the ones that actually generate Qi, to flow down and around the environment. From its highest peaks, Qi flows down to permeate the land, animating all life force, and finally stopping at the lowest point of the ground – where water ultimately collects. Subsequently, water, being the 'father', activates this very Qi.

Like all 'mothers', the function of mountains and hills are manifold. Not only do they generate Qi, but mountains also 'protect' areas from wind. Because wind disperses Qi, mountains can form a barricade to contain and circulate Qi withinin an area. In other words, very windy areas have few, or no mountains at all! In advanced Landform Feng Shui studies, mountain ranges that surround any area are called 'Embraces' – a 'Spiral City' is formed when multiple layers of embraces surround the land. The Qi collected in these areas are powerful and long-lasting.

Mountain, Water – or Both?

山管人丁
Mountains governs people

水管财
Water governs wealth

When deciding on a good Feng Shui area, we always try to look for both. Because 'mountains governs people; water governs wealth'. People aspects include health, relationships – and also power and authority. To answer your question 'which is more important? Mountain or water?', I personally choose mountain, simply because water you can create (see 'Your Aquarium Here' by Joey Yap!). Mountains you cannot create. Further more, mountains are the actual source of Qi, and it's always good to be near the source.

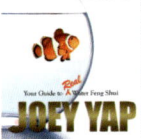

Of course, having said that, a superior Feng Shui site always comes with both mountain and water – natural ones, mind you.

Mountainology

The shape of mountains is not formed by random or by accident. There is a certain Tao to it. Over thousand of years, as the Earth orbits around the stars and planets, there is a certain interaction of energy. The stars that cross the same path over the Earth will have a gravitational pull on the surface of the Earth, over time. Internally when the underground tectonic plates of the Earth moves, it pushes the ground to rise upwards, and it settles into a shape or form that corresponds to the passing stars above in the sky.

For example, if it were a Fire star crossing the same path over thousand of years, a Fire shaped mountain would rise over that part of the Earth. If it were a Metal star in the sky crossing, then up grows a Metal shaped mountain. This is called the interaction, or correlation, between Heaven (stars) and Earth. What the shapes mean and how they look like – will be covered in Chapter 3 later.

While there are various classics – even so-called 'secret texts' – on water Feng Shui formulas, there are none for mountains. It is not because that mountains are unimportant, but it is because mountains are a *given* in Feng Shui. It is assumed to be there. So here's a Feng Shui secret that nobody ever told you – most Feng Shui formulas cannot work without the proper presence of mountains. And this includes the legendary 'Five Ghost Carry Treasure' formula.

Mountains and Your Bed

What do mountains have to do with your bed? After all, this entire book is dedicated to optimum bed location and placement.

They both share the same concept: Mountain are Yin; beds are also the Yin component for internal Feng Shui. Mountains govern health, relationships, power; and so too, for beds when located in the right sector, health, relationship, and/or power is enhanced. The location for ideal bed placement is largely based on the 'Sitting Star' of any Flying Star chart (more explained in Chapter 3); the 'Sitting Star' corresponds to the available mountains externally.

Here's another tip: beds should be as stable and as supported as possible because it is a Yin component (whereas doors are Yang). Hence, beds that are placed against glass windows or directly across from your room door – not good.

Chapter 2:
Feng Shui Rules for the Bed

2 Feng Shui Rules for the Bed

When it comes to internal Feng Shui – the Bed represents the characteristics of what a mountain would represent externally. Hence, a properly located bed would not only support good health to the occupants, but also bolster good relationships, and sometimes, contribute to elevation of social status, respect, and authority.

How this book is written, so you would later see, is primarily based on the unique Flying Star chart of your house. More details given in Chapter 4 on how to determine your house's Flying Star chart. And to take that one step further, some of the various sectors come with special effects – especially when supported externally by a hill of mountain. Of course, in case you're wondering, the mountain has to be visible from your bedroom to have actual effect.

Before we go into the details, here are some basic ground-rules that need to be observed for all bedrooms, irregardless.

Bed Rule #1:
A Waterbed is NOT a Bed.

One of my Feng Shui students thought he was quite clever, by 'combining' water with mountain – in a form of a waterbed. This obviously missed the mark. Think about it, a bed is supposed to be Yin – stable like a mountain. A waterbed is hardly that! Feng Shui is all about balance. Internally, the door governs Yang, while bedroom govern Yin. You need both to be good in order for the occupants to be optimally healthy and wealthy. What we don't need is a case of Yin-Yang imbalance! （陰陽失調） Especially in today's modern, extra stressful lifestyle, a goodnight's sleep is often what makes or breaks a person.

Of course, if your waterbed is not your daily, actual resting bed, and more for occasional leisure – then it's alright.

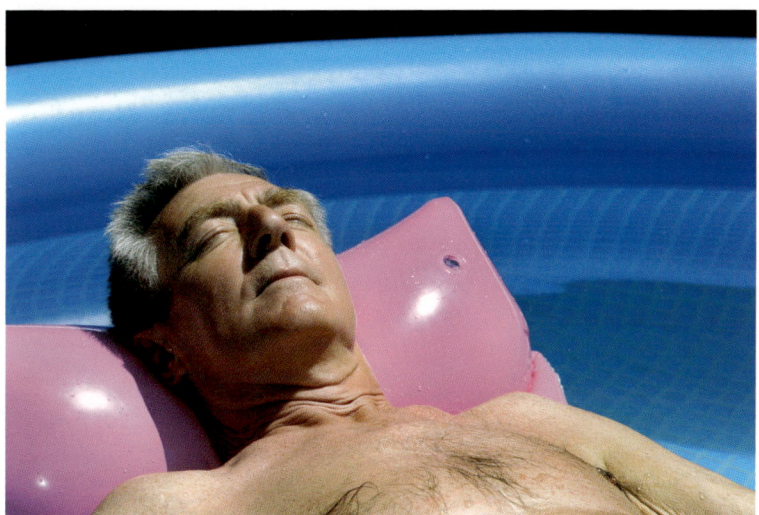

Your Head Here

Bed Rule #2:
Bed Against Solid Wall, Please.

How many times must a Feng Shui consultant repeat this – bed head to be placed against solid wall. The reason is simple enough: a wall that is solid supports the "Yin-ess" of the bed – lending it power, if you may. A match.

A bed that rests against a window is considered 'seeing Yang'. The quality of this bed is thus diminished. Worse still, some of the 'modern' bedrooms today comprises of glass panel walls on all sides. This is too Yang to be considered a fruitful resting place. The least to be done is to cover all unnecessary glass panels or windows with heavy drapes, when sleeping. This can help restore some Yin-factor to the bedroom.

Bed Rule #3:
Bed Material – Immaterial

Material is not a major concern. Your bed could be made of metal, wood, plastic – as long as the entire bed frame is stable. Do not be overly concerned that the Chinese word for 'bed' is written as '床', containing the 'wood' character inside.

Nor is the color of the bed awfully important. You can choose any color you like, just so long as it is pleasing to your eyes. After all, you are the one sleeping on it every night. There is <u>no such thing</u> as a 5-Element bed either! If you need more Fire element in your BaZi chart does not mean your bed (sheets) have to be red; green on the bed does not bring you 'more Wood Qi'. Having a wooden bed also does <u>not</u> give you 'more Wood Qi'.

Speaking about being solid, a bed should not have wheels. No matter how 'unique' your bedroom preferences are, a wheeled bed belongs only in the hospital, not your home.

Bed Rule #4:
Most Favorable Direction – Not

Many of you may have already studied your personal good directions based on your Life Gua (which is not covered in the scope of this book). Here are some of the common mistakes usually made:

Firstly, your favorable direction requires you to place your bed head against a window. That is not acceptable. Meaning, it is still better to face a negative Life Gua direction that allows you a solid wall – Yin supported by Yin. And also, you may have heard this before, 'Forms before Formula'. This tells us that the physical forms must first be qualified positively (hence, the need for this chapter), before matching with the formulas of Feng Shui (whether Life Gua, Flying Star, or others).

Here is one of my favorite bedroom blunders:

In order to point your bed head to your favorable direction, it requires you to place it at the 45 degree angle of the room corner. This is not only wrong, but it is also <u>BAD</u>. Effectively, this creates a triangle Fire–Sha (killings) – and your bed is tapping into this Sha. Expect restless nights, arguments, ill health – and in severe cases – divorce.

Maybe you think you can 'cover' this by creating a build-in cabinet to camouflage the 45 degree angle. But surely you realize the cabinet is also a triangular in shape – still a Fire-Sha.

Bed Rule #5:
Bedroom Shape is Regular.

The best shape for a bedroom would be regularly shaped, like a square or rectangular. As the room is the container for Qi, a squarish room allows Qi to flow evenly and stably.

Consequently, attic rooms that have the roof slanted are not considered ideal for flow of Qi. Rooms with triangular roofs upwards are also unsentimental.

Bed Rule #6:
Avoid Beams.

Almost everyone has heard of this one – avoid sleeping directly under a ceiling beam. This irregularity disrupts the flow of Qi from above you – sometimes directing Qi towards the sleeping you.

The most ideal remedy for this would be to create a false ceiling or plaster ceiling to cover-up the protrusion. Where that is not possible, move the bed away from being directly beneath the beam.

Bed Rule #7:
Bed room Poison Arrows.

When Feng Shui first started becoming more well-known, poison arrows seemed to be everywhere. Suddenly everyone was being 'stabbed from the back', or 'stabbed from the front'. To clear your doubts on 'poison arrows', understand that only angles of substantial size would constitute a poison arrow. For example, a wall corner (which is part of the building structure) is a real poison arrow. Your neighbor's entire slanted building corner angled towards you – that's a big poison arrow.

But those racks where your books and CD's sit-on – probably won't kill you.

So what happens if you are faced with this situation? :

Normally, placing something to block the view (and thus, the angle itself) like a plant or cabinet would do the trick.

Bed Rule #8:
Avoid Room Door towards Bed.

Whenever possible, we do not want the bed to be positioned directly aligned with the room door.

This is because Qi that comes into the room via the room door travels directly to hit the bed as it enters. Movement of Qi is Yang, thus affecting once again the *Yin-ness* of the bed.

Sometimes, the bed is located in the path of the toilet door. However, I feel this is not a serious situation. Think about it: does Qi come IN from the bathroom or toilet? Truth is, it does not. Qi only enters through the room door, and not the toilet door.

So as long as your bathrooms are cleaned, smells good, and you keep the bathroom door closed most of the time – no problem.

Bed Rule #9: Bedroom See Mountain.

This is not an actual rule in itself, but bedrooms that have a view of mountains externally have an added boost to it. As explained before, mountains are the source of Yin, whereas beds are the Yin components for internal Feng Shui. So when your bedroom itself sees a beautiful, lush mountain outside – this is a supported and good bedroom.

Of course, there a slight exceptions to this rule. Certain sectors prefer large mountains, while some are sufficient to see just higher ground outside. The overall quality of a mountain will be discussed in the following chapter.

So here's a trade secret for you – if, after you've finished this entire book but failed to understand anything from Chapter 5 onwards – come back to Bed Rule #9. Locate your bed in the bedroom that oversees a nice beautiful mountain. You cannot go that wrong with this one.

But of course, that would mean you missing out on some of the 'special effects' we'll be talking about….

Your Head Here

2

Feng Shui Rules for the Bed

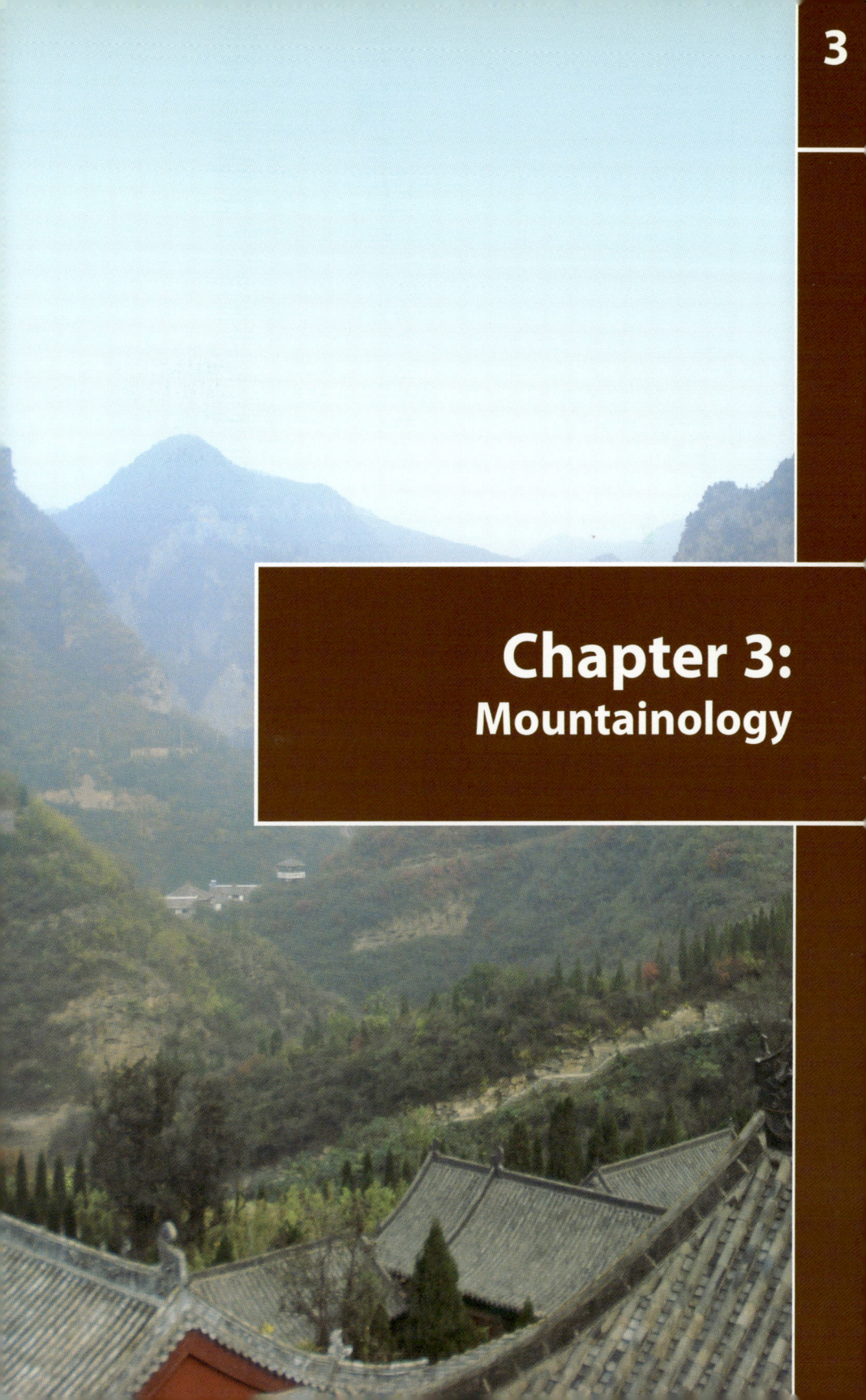

Chapter 3:
Mountainology

Mountainology

This chapter talks a little more on mountains, the natural Yin component of the lands. Are hills considered as mountains? The answer is Yes. A hill is a smaller mountain. Advanced practitioners are also well-accustomed to observing higher ground that represent 'very small hills', especially in areas that are relatively flat. This is a Landform study called 'Flatland Dragons'.

If you have not read the book '*Feng Shui For Homebuyers: Exterior*', you may not know what are deemed as good mountains and bad mountains.

Basically, mountains that generate positive, sentimental Qi to its vicinity are lush, green, and healthy-looking. Mountains that are rocky, patchy, or broken generate aggressive Qi.

In the previous chapter, I have stated that rooms that have a view of a good mountain or hill would be a <u>generally good</u> room. On the other hand, if your room overlooks an ugly, rocky mountain – it is <u>not</u> a good room!

Natural VS Manmade

Buildings are not mountains, very simple because they do not generate Qi. Buildings do not generate Qi because they are not born of the Earth, through the interaction between Heaven and Earth for thousands of years. Buildings might redirect Qi, or Sha Qi (killing force) sometimes, when angled sharply towards you.

But of course, for the sake of technical argument, you can 'build' a mountain. Firstly, it has to be at least 3 storeys high, or more. Secondly, it requires time for Qi to be incepted into this 'mountain'. After all, all substantially-sized physical matter can act as a container for Qi. But give it about 10 to 20 years before you can expect any effect….

3

Mountainology

In the study of Landforms Feng Shui, mountains can come in a form of a range (Dragon), wrap around an area to form an 'Embrace', or stand somewhat independently as a generator of Qi (called also a 'Star'). These 'Mountain Stars' can exist in one of the 5 element shapes. For example, a dome-shaped mountain belongs to the element of Metal; a wavy shaped mountain emits Water element Qi.

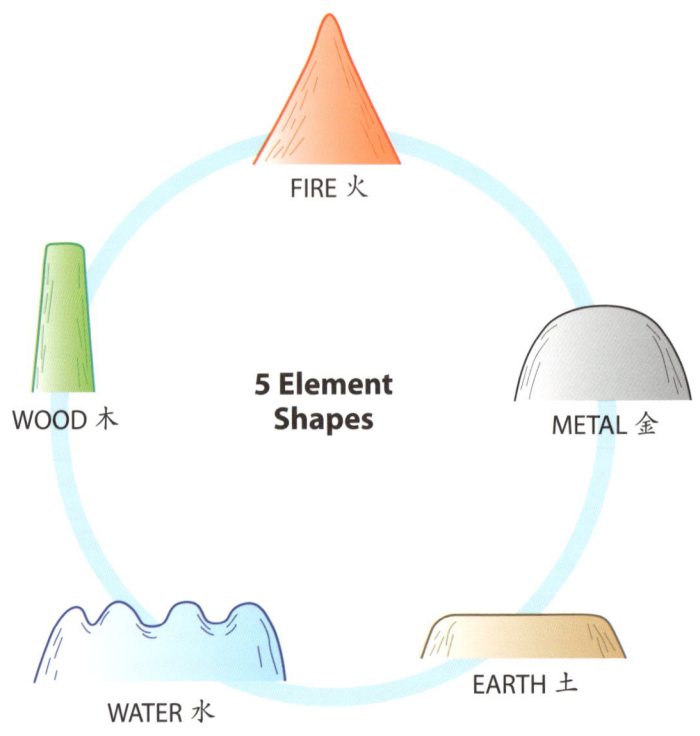

22   Your Head Here

Bedroom-ology

Look at your bedroom and bed locations as the 'mountain' within your house. Is it stable, protected, nurturing?

- Do you feel relaxed, safe, walking into your bedroom?

- Do you wake-up feeling refreshed, ready to take on the world? (and to make more money?)

- Do the relationships around you, especially at home, recharge you with a feeling of hope and gratitude?

These are signs that your bedroom is located in a positive sector. However, note the following:

- Do you wake-up feeling drained and tired the next morning?

- Do your friends constantly remind you to rest and relax more, that you look constantly tired?

- Are you constantly snappish and see the hopeless side of life?

- Is your sex life sluggish, dull – or even non-existent?

These are some of the signs that your bedroom is located in a negative sector. Or perhaps the internal Forms of your bedroom are not ideal. Check if there are too many glass windows, too many doors in your room – flip through Chapter 2 once again.

3

Mountainology

Chapter 4:
Using This Book

Using This Book

This book is meant for beginners in Feng Shui, and also useful for prospective homebuyers looking for a fuss-free way to plan their bedrooms and bed locations. All houses in the world need to have bedrooms (as much as their doors and bathrooms), but having said that, you may come across certain houses that have sub-standard internal Feng Shui potential – meaning, the Flying Stars chart simply does not allow a superior bedroom. Do not be alarmed – nor do you need to sell off the house right away. The 'secret' to dealing with these house charts lie in Chapter 2's Bed Rule #9.

Also in such cases, another thing you can do is to use Water Feng Shui (Your Aquarium Here) to make-up for the lack of mountain Feng Shui.

Your Bed Here

So how do you ascertain which Flying Star chart to use for your house? Here are some simple tasks for you to follow now. The good news is you only have to do it once…. for every house you own, that is.

- Ascertaining the Facing Direction of your home
- Demarcating the interior of your home according to the 8 Directions (North, South, East, West, Northeast, Northwest, Southeast, Southwest) – this is applicable to both landed properties and apartments
- Identifying your property's Flying Star chart to determine the most suitable location for a bed in your room

In this section, I will show you how to do all of the above (you'll see it's actually really easy). And then after that it's simply a matter of finding a bed you like, and putting it in the place it needs to be.

Ascertaining the Facing Direction of your home

If you have read some of Joey Yap's books like *Feng Shui for Homebuyers*, you should be quite familiar with taking a direction. For those who live in apartments, the process is slightly different - you may want to read *Feng Shui for Apartment Buyers* if you find you are having some trouble taking a direction for your apartment building as the subject is expansively dealt with in Feng Shui for Apartment Buyers.

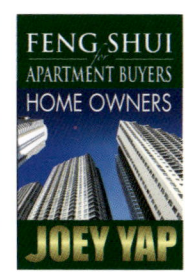

To find out the Facing Direction of your home, be it landed property or an apartment, you will need a compass. You do not need to use a Luo Pan – a scout's compass will do. The best is an automatic compass as it is not confusing and very easy to use.

Step 1: Find the Facing of your Home

The Facing of your home is the direction in which your home has been built to face. The best guide of the direction in which the home has been built to face is to look at the façade. If the façade is not obvious, then ascertain which is the most Yang side of the property. The most Yang side of the property is defined as the property which receives the most light, or which faces a main or busy street or road. That is usually the Facing when the façade is not obvious.

Do not use the location of the Main Door as an indication of the Facing of your home as there are many instances where the Main Door does not share the Facing of the building.

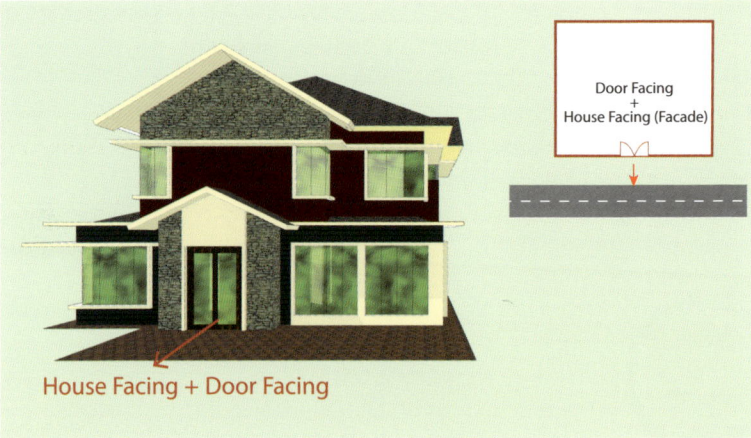

The house facing and the door facing are the same direction.

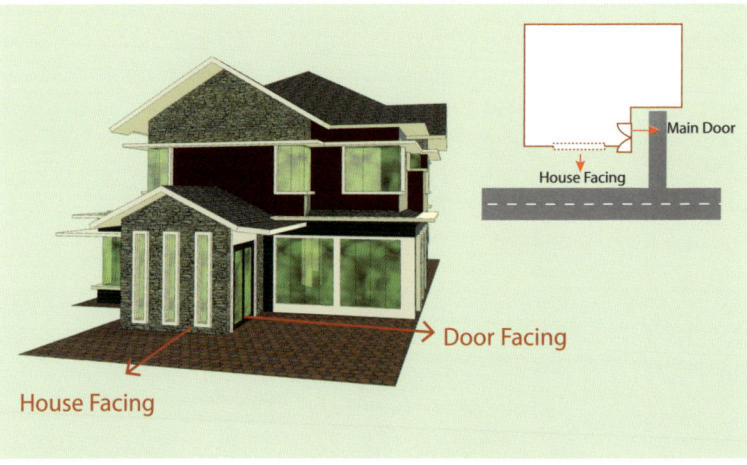

Don't assume that the Main Door always indicates the facing of the house; this illustration shows you an example of when the house facing and door facing are not in the same direction.

Step 2: Stand at the Facing of the property, with your back to the property. Hold up the compass and ascertain the Facing Direction of the property. In Classical Feng Shui, there are 24 possible Facing Directions, as each of the 8 basic directions are trisected into 3 sub-sectors. So a property doesn't just face say, East, it can have a East 1, East 2 or East 3 Facing Direction.

Check the list below to ascertain which is the Facing Direction of your property, based on the degrees of the compass. If you use a Luo Pan or my Mini-Compass, you won't need to refer to this chart.

Gua	Direction		24 Mountains			Degrees
離 Li	South	S1	Bing	丙	Yang Fire	157.6 - 172.5
		S2	Wu	午	Horse (Yang Fire)	172.6 - 187.5
		S3	Ding	丁	Yin Fire	187.6 - 202.5
坤 Kun	Southwest	SW1	Wei	未	Goat (Yin Earth)	202.6 - 217.5
		SW2	Kun	坤	South West (Earth)	217.6 - 232.5
		SW3	Shen	申	Monkey (Yang Metal)	232.6 - 247.5
兌 Dui	West	W1	Geng	庚	Yang Metal	247.6 - 262.5
		W2	You	酉	Rooster (Yin Metal)	262.6 - 277.5
		W3	Xin	辛	Yin Metal	277.6 - 292.5
乾 Qian	Northwest	NW1	Xu	戌	Dog (Yang Earth)	292.6 - 307.5
		NW2	Qian	乾	North West (Metal)	307.6 - 322.5
		NW3	Hai	亥	Pig (Yin Water)	322.6 - 337.5
坎 Kan	North	N1	Ren	壬	Yang Water	337.6 - 352.5
		N2	Zi	子	Rat (Yang Water)	352.6 - 7.5
		N3	Gui	癸	Yin Water	7.6 - 22.5
艮 Gen	Northeast	NE1	Chou	丑	Ox (Yin Earth)	22.6 - 37.5
		NE2	Gen	艮	North East (Earth)	37.6 - 52.5
		NE3	Yin	寅	Tiger (Yang Wood)	52.6 - 67.5
震 Zhen	East	E1	Jia	甲	Yang Wood	67.6 - 82.5
		E2	Mao	卯	Rabbit (Yin Wood)	82.6 - 97.5
		E3	Yi	乙	Yin Wood	97.6 - 112.5
巽 Xun	Southeast	SE1	Chen	辰	Dragon (Yang Earth)	112.6 - 127.5
		SE2	Xun	巽	South East (Wood)	127.6 - 142.5
		SE3	Si	巳	Snake (Yin Fire)	142.6 - 157.5

Your Head Here

Demarcating the Interior of your Home

The purpose of demarcating the interior of your home is to enable you to determine which rooms or areas of your home fall within which one of the 8 directions. To do this you will need:

- Floor plan of your home (preferably an architect or draftsman's version)
- Red pen and a ruler

The interior of a property is always demarcated using the nine grids method. Here is how you do it:

Step 1: Super-impose the Nine Grids over your property floor plan.

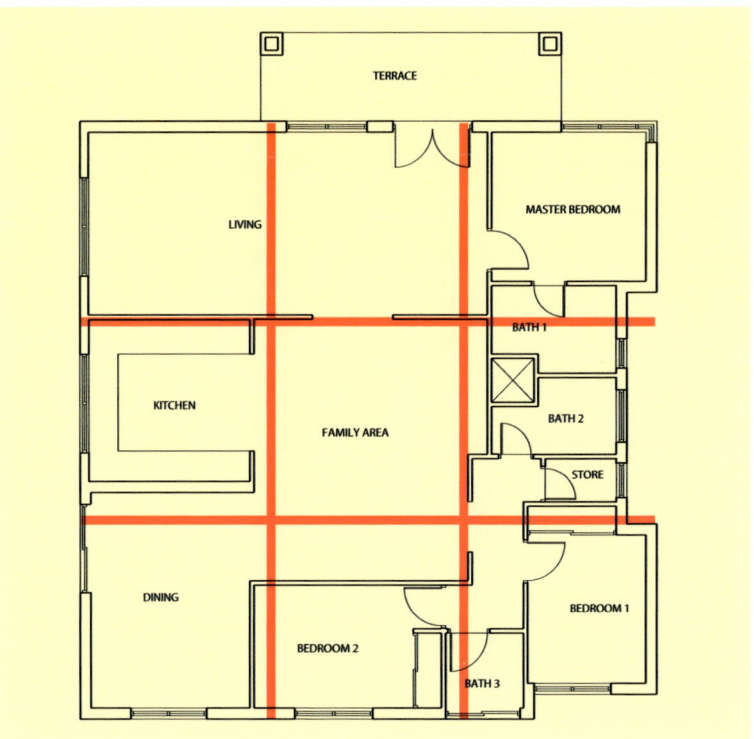

Step 2: Mark the Facing Direction in the center square of the grid where the front of your home is located. For example, if your home faces East (either East 1, 2, or 3), mark East in the center square of the three squares that correspond with the front of your property.

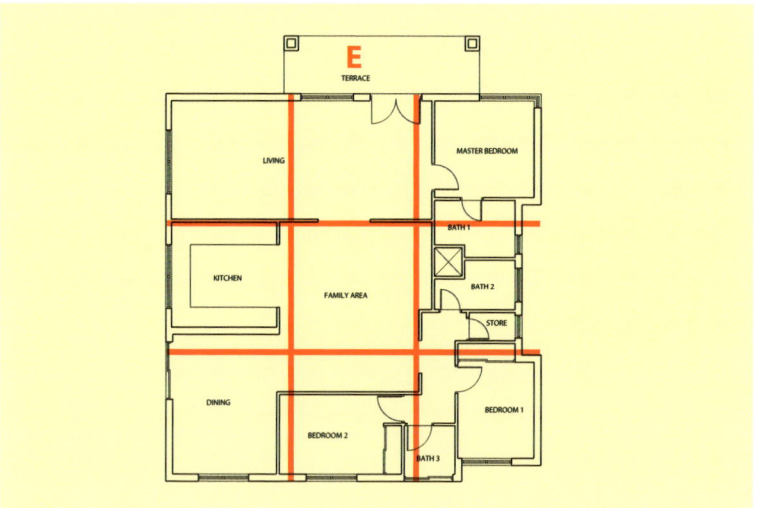

Step 3: Mark out the rest of the directions in an orderly, clock-wise fashion.

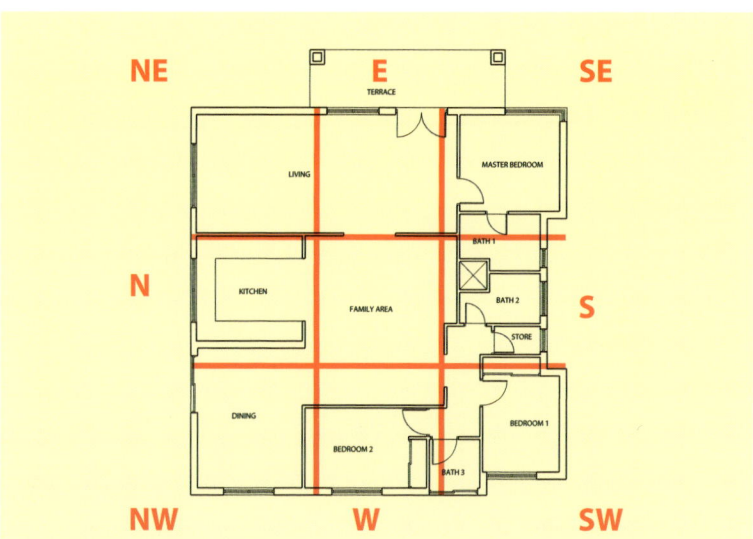

You should now be able to determine which section or area or room in your home, corresponds with each of the 8 Directions.

Identifying the Flying Star Chart of your property

Based on the Facing Direction of your property, find the relevant Flying Star chart in the pages overleaf.

For ease of reference, the charts are divided up into Period 7 properties and Period 8 properties. How do you know which period is applicable to your property?

> If you moved into your home between **1984 - 2003**, then your property is a Period 7 property. All the charts relevant to Period 7 properties are located at page 47.
>
> If you moved into your home between **2004 – 2023**, then your property is a Period 8 property. All the charts relevant to Period 8 properties are located at page 81.

Apartments and Move-In Dates

The move-in date is only used to determine the chart of the property when it is landed property being considered. In the case of apartments, the date that you moved into the apartment is not the correct reference. Instead, you should use the date in which the apartment building was first occupied.

If you are living in a relatively new apartment building (completed say, after 2004) and you are one of the early occupants or original owners, then use the date you moved in. If you are living in an apartment building that was completed between 1984 - 2003, but you only moved into the building in 2005, DO NOT use the date you moved in. Your property would be considered a Period 7 building, so use the charts relevant to Period 7, not Period 8.

Now that you found the Qi map (Flying Star chart) of your property, refer to the corresponding page and you will discover the best location(s) to place your bed at. Firstly, it tells you which sector or room is the best – and guess what? It is not always your master bedroom or the biggest available room.

If it happens that one of the prescribed positive bedroom sectors are available to use as a room, then perfect. Like I said, it might not be the biggest room, but it is a good room.

Small Tai Ji

Now that you have identified the right room, what next? Some of the commentaries also include something called 'Small Tai Ji'. This states that within the prescribed room, you can further demarcate another 9 Palace Grid.

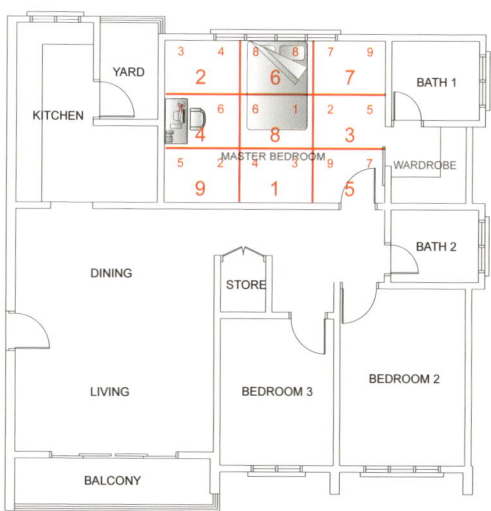

So when it states, the best room is in the Northeast sector and to place your bed at the North Small Tai Ji (or sub-sector) – this means that the most ideal location inside the Northeast room for the bed would be in the Northern corner.

Technically Speaking

Admittedly, some houses allow you to dwell on the finer details, whereas some do not. When it becomes too complicated, take a step back, take a deep breath, and have a go at it again later.

For those who are initiated into the mechanics of Feng Shui, you will be able to derive more from the Flying Star chart yourself; then the commentaries become more of a reference guide to you. You may agree, you may not sometimes. Of course, being a Feng Shui practitioner myself, it is not substantial to base your recommendations on just the Flying Stars. If you are familiar with Bed Rule #9, then you will see that external mountain forms will be able to supersede the internal Flying Stars <u>most of the time</u>. After all, San He Landform Feng Shui happen to be one of my favorite topics as well. But due to the limitations (and size) of this book, much of the very technical aspects are omitted.

In some cases, you might get a glimpse or the application of San He's '3 Auspicious, 6 Elegance' 三吉六秀 coming into play for certain houses. Try as I may, not all house charts qualify for this.

San He

San Yuan

And last but definitely not least, no San Yuan system (as Flying Stars is) will be complete without considering the very crucial 'Direct-Indirect Spirit Locations' 零正神位. While this has nothing to do with ghosts and other magical spirits, it certainly is an important consideration on a macro view point. This is also why in some cases you will see that not all Sitting Star #8, #9, or #1 is employed for their so-called 'always positive' characteristics. Sometimes, they can get cranky too.

The Limitations of This Book.

This is a self-help Feng Shui book, so before you run off to find a contractor to remove your existing bedroom, and swap sectors with the toilet – hold your horses! Consider if there are any other rooms you can use. Consider if there are external support from mountains or hills. Consider if your existing bedroom is really, really bad for you.

Often times we are so focused on what we cannot do, we forget about what we can do. Is there a Small Tai Ji within your existing bedroom that you can use? Or is the other, smaller room more suited for your current needs and life-goals?

This book is not written to instill fear in you. Feng Shui should not be a fearful subject. If you do not adhere to it, no one is going to get hurt (not unless you activate the very negative #5 Yellow, that is). But I see it as a wonderful tool to make life easier, better, and more fulfilling, too. Sometimes, even that slightest touch of good health, or improving generally all the relationships around you, can make world of a difference.

And finally, if the going gets too tough – get help from a professional Feng Shui practitioner. Feng Shui is like fixing a car sometimes. Not everybody enjoys it. But everyone sure would like to own one.

To keep things simple, I have also limited the charts to Period 7 and Period 8 homes as in my experience, these are the majority of the properties that are out there. This does mean that if your house is a Period 6 or pre-Period 6 property, the content of this book will not be applicable to you. You may therefore wish to seek the assistance of a Feng Shui consultant if you wish to utilise Feng Shui in your home or property.

4

Chapter 5:
HOMES FACING IN PERIOD 7

South 1 (丙) Facing Homes in Period 7

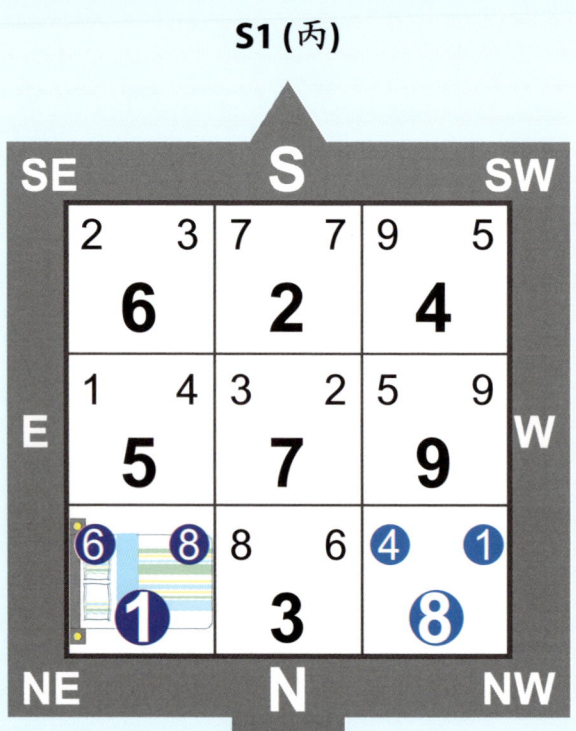

Where do you put your bed?

Best Location	Northeast
2nd Best Location	Northwest

Your Head Here

Commentary

A South 1 facing property, Period 7, has only two auspicious bedroom sectors. The first is the Northeast sector. The #6 and #8 Stars in this room promote good health, stability as well as power and authority. This room is especially beneficial for those in managerial positions like CEO's and Department Leaders. Ones reputation is also augmented by using this bedroom, especially when the external ground is higher. In the occasion where a Metal shaped mountain is present externally then this room enhances political power. When using this room, it is preferred to face the East direction, instead of North.

The Northwest sector is a Peach Blossom sector. As such, you must ensure that there are no negative features externally, such as a lamp post, dead tree, or an overly active road. In its positive form, the stars here promotes intelligence, good connections and attractiveness - making this suitable for those in sales, PR, entertainment or generally the people business.

Another usable option would be a South bedroom. However, #7 Star in this sector is not in its entirely positive form. What you can do is to place your bed in the Eastern Small Tai Ji of the room. This will enable the #7 Star to exert its positive influence such as good communication skills, precision, and strategy. Generally, when your bedroom contains both the Southeast and South sectors, it is still considered a positive bedroom to use. Allow the Qi to flow from South to Southeast by ensuring there is no physical wall or partition in between these sectors.

5 South 2 (午) or South 3 (丁) Facing Homes in Period 7

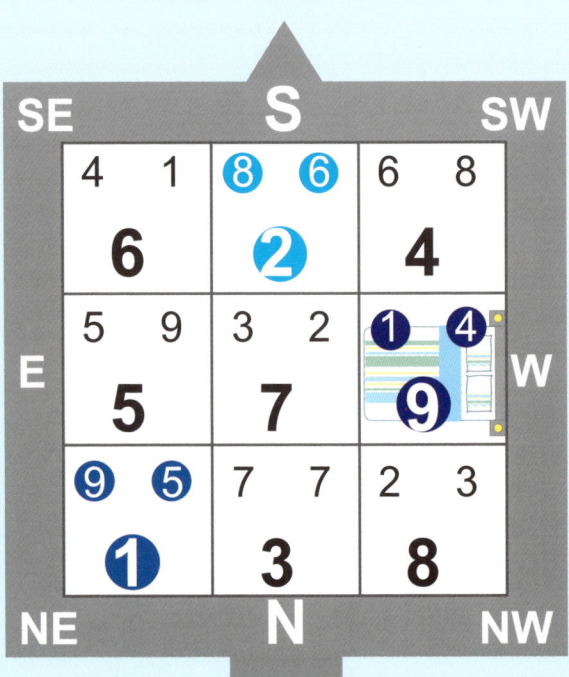

Where do you put your bed?

Best Location	West
2nd Best Location	Northeast
3rd Best Location	South

Commentary

A Period 7 South 2/South 3 facing property has three positive sectors for bedrooms. The first option is the West sector, which contains the Literary Formation 1-4. Hence this room is suitable for those in the education business, creativity and design, writing and fine arts. Additionally this formation also helps promote ones good name and influence. This is especially true when there is higher ground in the Western external. Locating your bed exactly on West 3 enhances the effects of nobility and elite social influence.

The Northeast room contains the Future Prosperous #9 Star. This room is generally beneficial for health and healing. Those in the beauty and relaxation industries, like spas and massage, will directly benefit by sleeping in this room. Take note however while this sector is beneficial for long term well being, occupants might find themselves feeling anxious and impatient initially. The best sub-sector for the bed location is Northeast 2, as measured from the center of the entire floor plan.

The third positive sector for this house is the South sector. The Stars in this room offers long term stability, calmness and peace of mind. This is a good room to meditate in. Avoid placing your bed in the East Small Tai Ji. The West Small Tai Ji would be most ideal for this South sector bedroom.

5 Southwest 1 (未) Facing Homes in Period 7

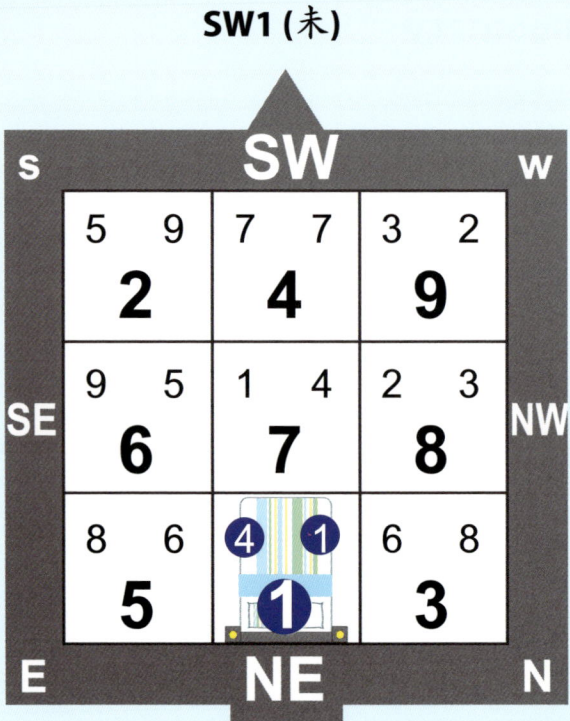

Where do you put your bed?

| Best Location | Northeast |

Commentary

A Southwest 1 facing house has primarily only one positive bedroom sector, which is the Northeast sector. This is the 1-4 combination in its stable form, which enhances ones intelligence, capacity to learn and investment acumen. As usual this combination also supports those in the education and writing industries, including printing, textile and traditional medicine. The best location for the bed is Northeast 2 or Northeast 3 within this room. Alternately, the Southeast Small Tai Ji is also acceptable for locating your bed head there.

All the remaining sectors are considered as average bedrooms. However, the South sector is considered least ideal, unless supported externally by a beautiful hill or mountain.

Southwest 2 (坤) or Southwest 3 (申) Facing Homes in Period 7

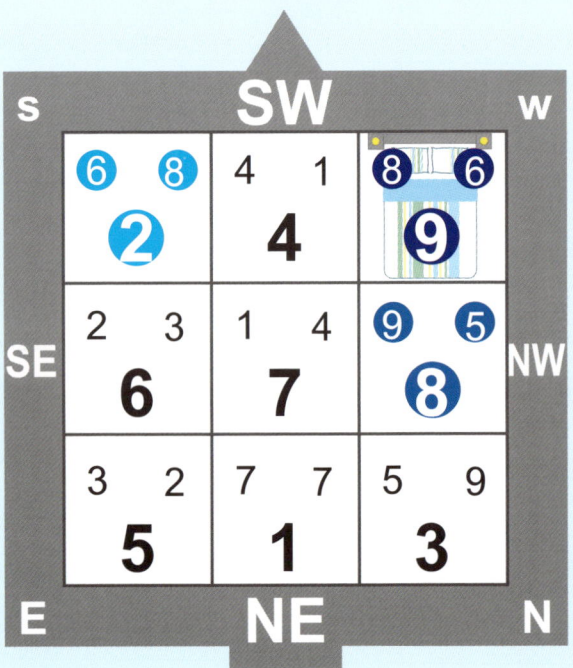

Where do you put your bed?

Best Location	West
2nd Best Location	Northwest
3rd Best Location	South

Your Head Here

Commentary

The best bedroom sector for this house is the West sector. The general positive effects are financial stability, good health and a balanced temperament. When matched with a mountain outside, this formation prolongs lifespan. The best location for the bed would be the Northwest Small Tai Ji, or the South Small Tai Ji.

The Northwest sector makes an excellent bedroom for those in the people business and the healing arts. This extends to any field that contributes to health and improvement of the human body. As for the exact bed location, use the Northwest Small Tai Ji or Southwest Small Tai Ji of this room for maximum benefit.

The third option for a positive bedroom is the South sector. The stars here enhance ones power and authority as well as overall health. Take note however that this sector is not ideal for Gua #6 persons – bringing along side effects such as migraine and backache when using this room. Ideally, one should use the Southwest Small Tai Ji of this room.

West 1 (庚) Facing Homes in Period 7

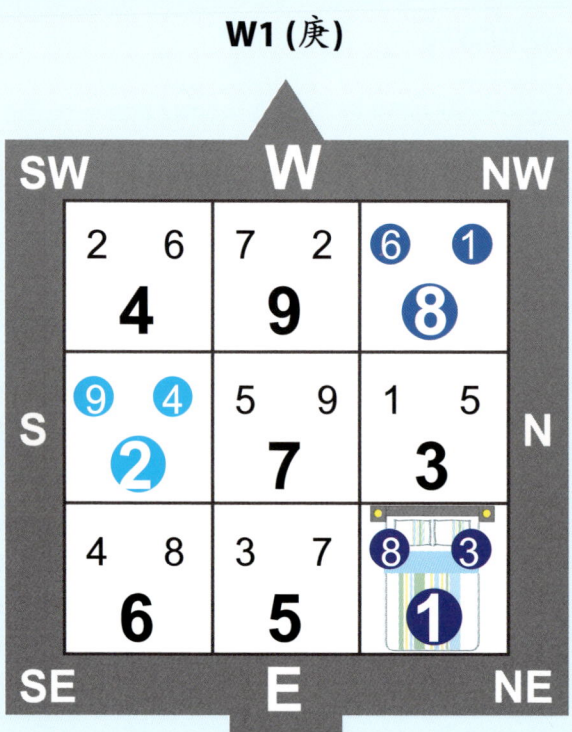

Where do you put your bed?

Best Location	Northeast
2nd Best Location	Northwest
3rd Best Location	South

Commentary

The most powerful room to use in a Period 7 Facing West 1 house is the Northeast sector. The Prosperous #8 Star returns to its own Palace. Along with good health and stability this room also offers financial luck, especially to those working in large organizations and multinational companies. Gua #3 persons using this room will reap more financial benefits but suffer side effects of back and joint aches. If there is a fire shaped mountain seen here externally, this room promotes spiritual peace, but this also means that this is not ideal for those seeking meaningful and adventurous relationships. All Small Tai Ji locations are acceptable for bed placement in this room.

The Northwest bedroom is excellent for those in sports, military and those in managerial positions as well. Using this room also enhances ones business intelligence and strategy. If there is a natural water body to the Northwest, then it renders the occupant of this room to become emotionally driven and impulsive. That being said, those in nocturnal profession will still benefit from this Feng Shui configuration. For this room, it is best used a Northern Small Tai Ji facing North.

The third positive room for the West 1 facing house is the South sector bedroom. Here is the future Prosperous Star, which promotes good health, high energy levels and good relationships. Gua #3 persons might find this room too hot to handle, meaning, impulsiveness and occasional heatiness. Gua #1 persons will benefit most by using this room. The Southwest, South, and the Southeast Small Tai Ji are all acceptable locations to have your bed at. If this room happens to open a Northwest Small Tai Ji room door, this is called a 'Prosperous Fire Receiving Water' formation – ushering powerful alliances and influence over large groups of people. This formation is further activated when there is a Greedy Wolf mountain in the Southern external.

West 2 (酉) or West 3 (辛) Facing Homes in Period 7

Where do you put your bed?

Best Location	South
2nd Best Location	Northwest

Commentary

There are only two positive bedroom sectors for a Period 7 West 2 / West 3 facing property. Primarily, the South sector is excellent for those running their own businesses. Those working in multinational organizations and conglomerates will also benefit by using this room. The Small Tai Ji of Southeast and Southwest are preferred.

The second best bedroom to use is the Northwest sector. This room is suitable for those in the education business, writing and printing business, as well as establishing teaching institutions of any kind. Overall, the health quality of this room is also good. Ensure that there is no busy road junction externally. If there is, then build a wall or plant tall trees to buffer the effect. For this Northwest bedroom, use the Small Tai Ji of either the North or South.

Northwest 1 (戌) Facing Homes in Period 7

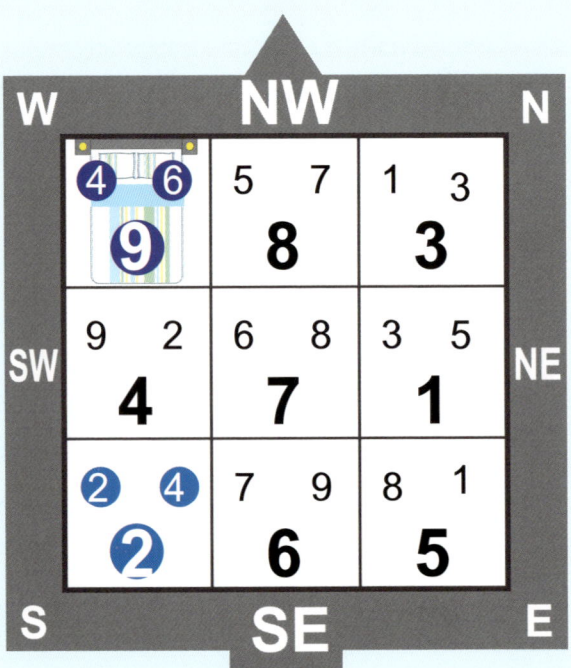

Where do you put your bed?

Best Location	West
2nd Best Location	South

Commentary

The West sector is generally acceptable to be used as a bedroom. The #4 Star here is weak, and therefore requires support from external higher ground, hill, or mountain. Having fulfilled that, then this room enhances both literary and military prowess. Use the Southwest Small Tai Ji to locate your bed.

Another acceptable bedroom to use is the South sector. Again, the #2 Star here should be supported by external mountain. Then, this room will be beneficial to those in the spiritual and metaphysics industries. Tap into the South 1 direction to enhance long term good health within this room.

For a Period 7 Northwest 1 facing property, essentially there are only two acceptable bedrooms. Failing which, the East sector can also be used as the second grade bedroom. Within this room, use the Northeast Small Tai Ji.

Northwest 2 (乾) or Northwest 3 (亥) Facing Homes in Period 7

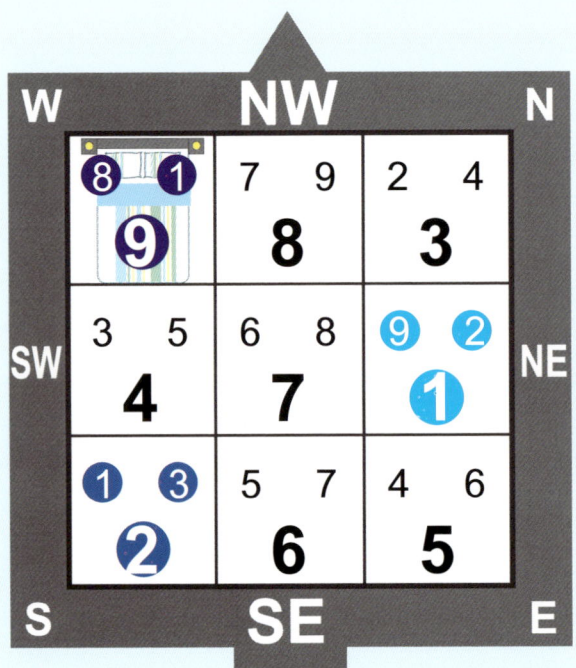

Where do you put your bed?

Best Location	West
2nd Best Location	South
3rd Best Location	Northeast

Commentary

For a Period 7 Northwest 2 / 3 facing house, the West sector makes a powerful bedroom. Aside from enhancing overall good health, this room also promotes lasting relationships – you will learn delightful new surprises from your spouse or partner every single day!
This allows all relationships to stay fresh without a dull moment. If that is not enough, the stars in this sector also enhance general wealth luck. It is of course even better when this sector is supported externally by a hill or mountain – further activating the positive effects of 'Mountain & Water Bliss'. All Small Tai Ji locations are acceptable for bed placement within this room.

The South sector room is excellent for those whose work involve constant travelling and moving around. The stars here ensure your vitality level is strengthened, at the same time promoting smooth wealth potential. Performers and public speakers will also benefit greatly by using this bedroom. This is however not a good room in terms of personal relationships due to its volatile nature. Avoid placing your bed in the Southeast Small Tai Ji.

Another powerful room available for a Period 7 Northwest 2 / 3 facing house is the Northeast sector. The formation here, if supported by positive external forms, promotes the natural healing abilities of the human body. This also means that those involved in medicine, healing, massage therapies, spa and relaxation centers will benefit the most when using this bedroom. Use the East Small Tai Ji for maximum effects. Additionally, if the room door opens at the South Small Tai Ji, this room fulfills the 'Wood & Fire Brilliance' formation – heralding the birth of an intelligent male child, along with constant flow of good news and tidings.

North 1 (壬) Facing Homes in Period 7

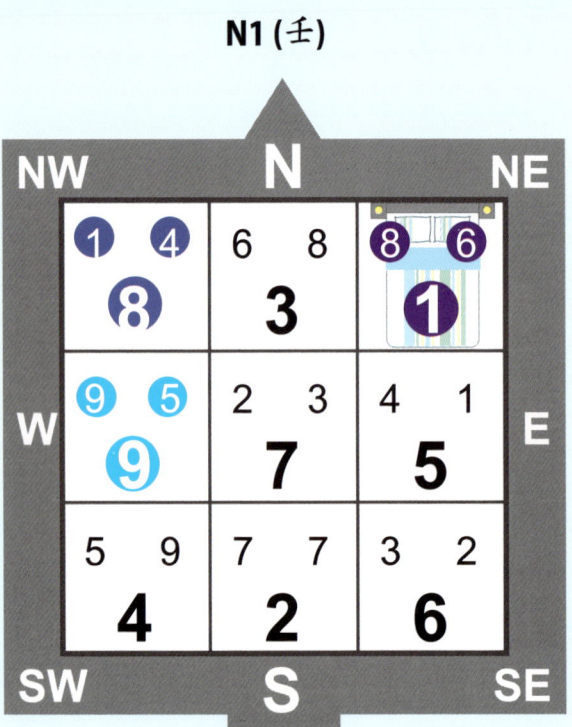

Where do you put your bed?

Best Location	Northeast
2nd Best Location	Northwest
3rd Best Location	West

Commentary

The Northeast sector is a very stable and prosperous to be used, promoting long term health and relationships. If there is higher ground externally, you cannot go wrong with this bedroom. If you see an Earth shaped mountain externally, this bedroom can also improve financial well being! This room is suitable for people of all Gua. Additionally, all Small Tai Ji locations are acceptable to place your bed at.

The next best bedroom is the Northwest sector. With the Literary Formation of 1-4 here, this room promotes good name and reputation. Those in creative arts, fine arts, writing and journalism, as well as those in service to others will find all their hard work recognized, appreciated, and awarded. This formation is further enhanced by using the East Small Tai Ji. Alternately, the West Small Tai Ji is also beneficial.

The West sector bedroom is perfect for those in the beauty and entertainment industries. If you are a wedding planner, fashion model, or make-up artist – this is the room for you! When not afflicted by negative forms, the energies of this room can help you build fame and respect over time. Avoid using the Southwest Small Tai Ji as well as the North Small Tai Ji for your bed. Overall, this room promotes good feelings and good health for its occupants.

North 2 (子) or North 3 (癸) Facing Homes in Period 7

Where do you put your bed?

Best Location	South
2nd Best Location	West

Commentary

The Period 7 North 2 / 3 facing house has two positive bedrooms. The South sector is the most stable bedroom, promoting health and vitality. When supported by a Metal shaped mountain externally, this room enhances power and authority. As a side effect though, such power comes with loneliness – not something you normally want for married couples, so take note. When supported by any other mountain or higher ground, there will not be any side effects. The positive effects are more pronounced for the North 3 facing house. Locate your bed in the Southeast or Southwest Small Tai Ji within this room.

The West sector bedroom has the Peach Blossom formation. Hence it should not be further activated by the presence of Water. Ensure that this sector is quiet and peaceful externally. When these conditions are met, this room promotes good health, intelligence and positive relationships. When supported externally by a hill, the occupant of this room will marry a powerful spouse. However, in the presence of overly Yang external conditions, there is opportunity to become embroiled in scandals and loss of reputation. In the rare event where a pool of dirty water is present externally, the occupants should be careful of sexually transmitted deceases.

Additionally, the Southeast sector can be used as a second grade bedroom, with minor positive effects. The ideal Small Tai Ji location is in the East.

Your Head Here

5 Northeast 1 (丑) Facing Homes in Period 7

NE1 (丑)

8 6 **3**	① ④ **①**	6 8 **5**
3 2 **8**	4 1 **7**	5 9 **6**
2 3 **9**	7 7 **4**	⑨ ⑤ **②**

N · NE · E · NW · SE · W · SW · S

Where do you put your bed?

Best Location	Northeast
2nd Best Location	South

Commentary

For a Period 7 Northeast 1 facing property, the Northeast sector itself is the most positive bedroom! Even when the Northeast sector joins with the East sector as one big bedroom, the positive effects are retained. Generally, this sector enhances good health, good name, and good relationships. Gua #2 persons receives slightly less benefits from this room. Avoid using the Southeast Small Tai Ji. Using the East Small Tai Ji enhances political reputation and business acumen.

The South sector is also an auspicious bedroom. This sector promotes general good health and happiness. When afflicted by Fire shaped negative forms, the occupants in this room will lean towards paranoia, obsessive behaviors, and skin decease. When supported externally by positive forms, this room brings great beauty and charisma to its occupants.

Northeast 2 (艮) or Northeast 3 (寅) Facing Homes in Period 7

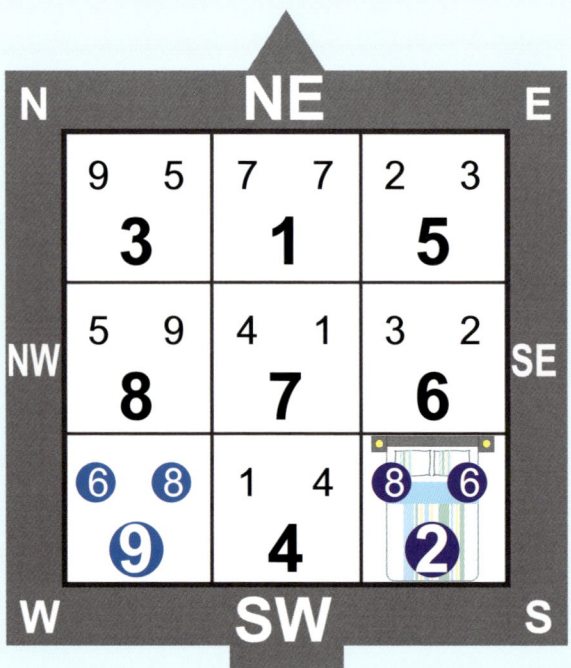

Where do you put your bed?

Best Location	South
2nd Best Location	West

Commentary

The Period 7 facing Northeast 2 / 3 house has two positive sectors of almost similar effect. The South sector contains the Prosperous #8 star, which directly promotes good health and a touch of property luck. If this sector is afflicted by negative forms, whether external or internal, the occupants may suffer from osteoporosis or hardening of the cells. Muscle stiffness might be an early warning symptom. While this sector is generally stable, it tends to lead to boredom in relationships especially during years when the annual Earth Star flies in. To negate this side effect, it is ideal to use the Southwest sub-sector for your bed location.

The second bedroom option for this house is the West sector, which contains the 6-8 White Stars. Alternately the Northeast sector is usable even though it is a second grade bedroom. It is still beneficial to specialists, dentists, surgeons as well as motivational speakers. If there is external water seen from this sector, then all positive attributes are diminished. A Wood shaped building here would conversely bring out the positive qualities of the #7 star. Good health is coupled with authority and staying power. When supported by external hills, this sector allows one to have power behind the scenes – like imperial advisors of ancient days. Avoid placing your bed in the Northwest Small Tai Ji of the room.

East 1 (甲) Facing Homes in Period 7

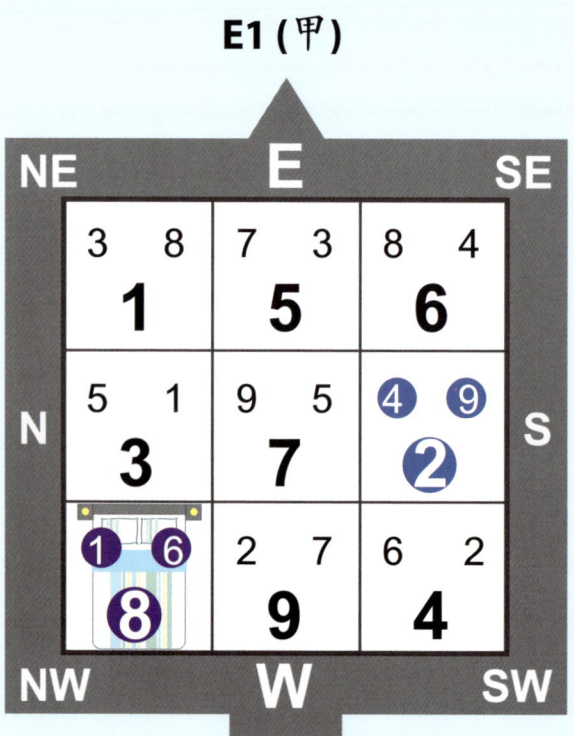

Where do you put your bed?

Best Location	Northwest
2nd Best Location	South

Commentary

The most powerful bedroom for this house is the Northwest sector. Here, all the three auspicious White Stars converge – enhancing good luck, career, and longevity. This bedroom can be beneficial whether you are self-employed or working for others. This is especially true when matched with a Southeast sub-sector. A Northwest mountain or hill will confer great recognition, respect, and power to the occupants of this room. In the Small Tai Ji, avoid using the North and West as they counter the positive effects of the White Stars.

The other positive bedroom is the South sector. However it is not beneficial for persons belonging to Gua #6 and #7. Seeing a Metal shaped mountain externally will bring immense power and respect to the occupant of this room. However, personal relationships tend to suffer, and there will be problems relating to the lungs and the head. Gua #1 and #4 persons are more suited to use this bedroom. The bed should be located in the Southeast Small Tai Ji.

The West sector room is usable only if the room door opens at Northeast Small Tai Ji. Failing which, the star configuration at this room has a potential for problems related to the lungs, brain and the womb.

5 East 2 (卯) or East 3 (乙) Facing Homes in Period 7

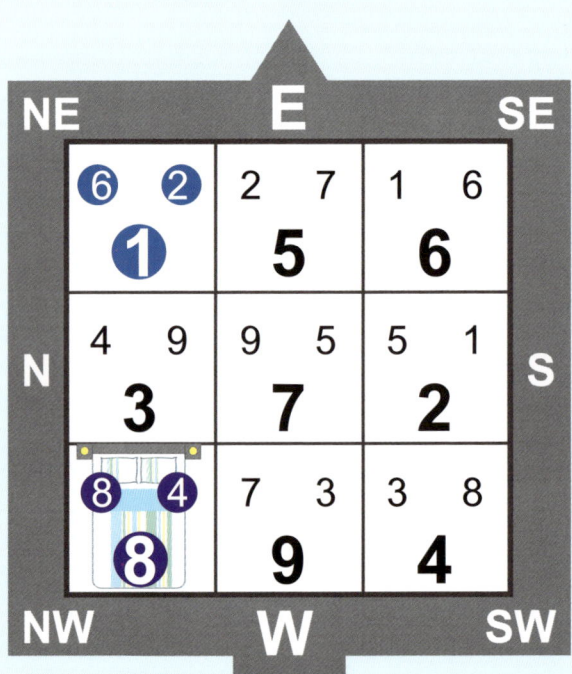

Where do you put your bed?

Best Location	Northwest
2ⁿᵈ Best Location	Northeast

Commentary

The Northwest sector is the best bedroom for a Period 7 East 2 / 3 facing property. The positive effects include good health, peace of mind, and overall calmness. One will also develop a taste for finer things in live when using this room. Those involved in creative endeavors, abstract art and all things culinary will directly benefit by using this room. On a side note, if the Northwest external is situated in a dead end road, or afflicted by merciless water forms – this sector causes potential for poisoning, paranoia, and in worst case scenario, insanity. When supported by positive external forms, the stars here enhance creativity and literary pursuits that can lead to great wealth.

The Northeast room is also considered auspicious. Those who are running their own business will be supported by this room. Those in the metal industry, such as automobile, banking, and all forms of machinery and manufacturing, will benefit from using this bedroom. Ideally, the bed should be located at North Small Tai Ji or the Southeast Small Tai Ji. If the Northeast is afflicted by a highway or fast moving water, then this room may cause hallucinations and depression to the occupants.

Southeast 1 (辰) Facing Homes in Period 7

PERIOD 7 — **SE1 (辰)**

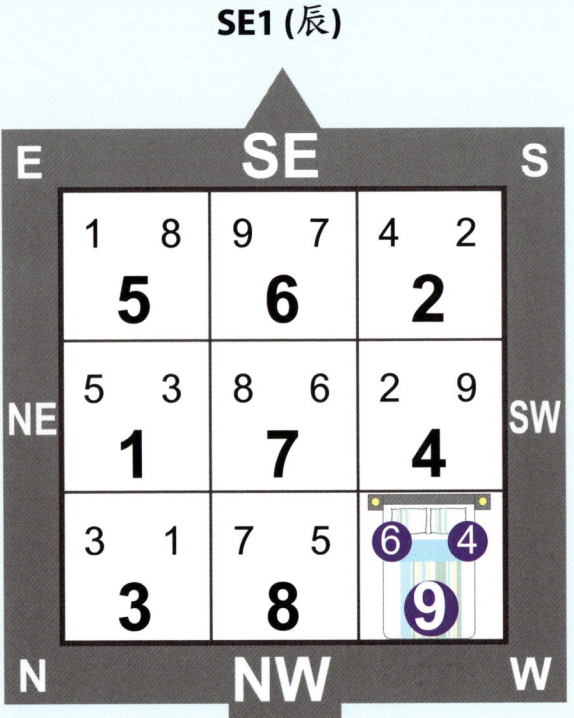

Where do you put your bed?

Best Location	West

Commentary

The Period 7 Southeast 1 facing house has only one stable bedroom sector – the West sector. This room promotes short term wealth and fast moving projects. While generally good for health, the occupant of this room tend to travel a lot as well. One should capitalize on this condition to generate money. When supported by external higher ground or hills, then this sector allows long term health and authority. The Small Tai Ji to use is the Southwest.

All remaining sectors are considered lesser grade bedrooms. The East sector can still be used, with minor positive qualities such as help from Noble people at work, and being recognized for all your efforts.

Southeast 2 (巽) or Southeast 3 (巳) Facing Homes in Period 7

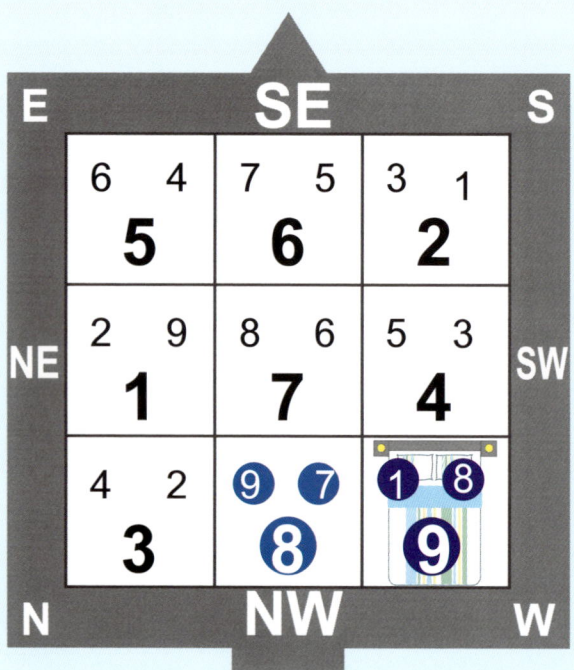

Where do you put your bed?

Best Location	West
2nd Best Location	Northwest

Commentary

The best sector available for this house is the West sector. A bedroom here not only ensures good health, but also helps generate money making ideas. This sector also supports professions dealing with animals, such as a veterinarian, and those in pet business. This room is also good for relationships and children's well being. Avoid using the Southwest Small Tai Ji. The most ideal bed location for this room is the Northwest Small Tai Ji.

The Future Prosperous Star #9 resides here in the Northwest sector, promising good health and relationships. This room has a touch of romance to it, making it a perfect bedroom for newly weds. Placing the bed in the South Small Tai Ji of this room can help the occupants in conceiving a child (coupled with Proper Date selection!). Gua #2 persons will reap maximum benefit from a Northwest bedroom.

As a second grade bedroom, the Northeast sector can also be used with the exception of Gua #1 persons.

5

Chapter 6:
HOMES FACING IN PERIOD 8

South 1 (丙) Facing Homes in Period 8

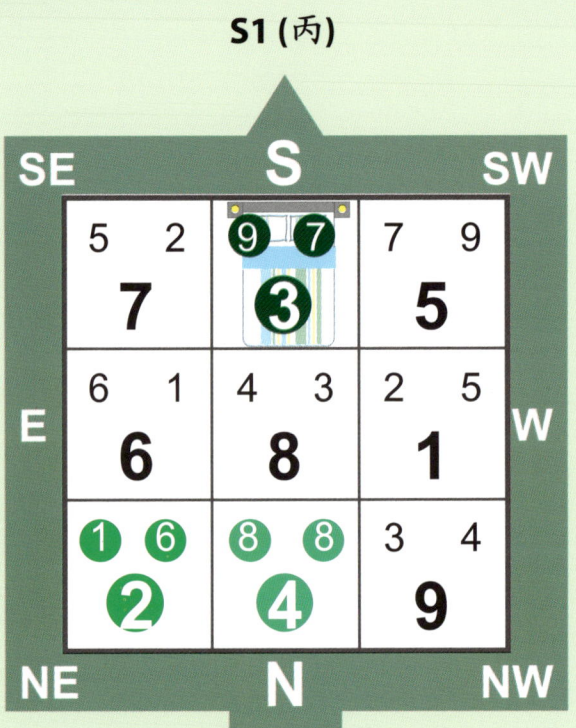

Where do you put your bed?

Best Location	South
2nd Best Location	Northeast
3rd Best Location	North

Commentary

The best bedroom for a Period 8 South 1 facing house happens to be the South sector itself. The stars here promote beauty and elegance, in addition to a robust health. Those involved in the beauty industry, public relations and entertainment will benefit by using this South sector bedroom. Seeing higher ground externally further enhances the positive qualities of this sector. Ideally place your bed in the South 3 sector of the 24 Mountains as measured from the centre of the property. This special configuration boosts fame and support from the public. Avoid using the Southeast sub-sector of this room. When afflicted by negative external forms such as a sharp roof point, then the occupants of this room risks being cheated by conmen or gold-diggers.

The Northeast sector bedroom is suitable for business owners and those in sales. When supported externally by positive forms, the occupants will constantly encounter helpful people in their lives. Ideally, the bed location should be at the East or North Small Tai Ji. Avoid using the Southeast Small Tai Ji as this counters the positive effects of the 1-6 HeTu Combination here.

The North sector which contains the double #8 Stars can also be used as a bedroom. However, this is considered as a second grade bedroom because it produces workaholics. Hence, it is unsuitable for elderly or retired folks.

South 2 (午) or South 3 (丁) Facing Homes in Period 8

S2 (午) / S3 (丁)

Where do you put your bed?

Best Location	West
2nd Best Location	South

Your Head Here

Commentary

The strongest bedroom for this house is the West sector. The stars here promotes intelligence, business wisdom and unconventional tactics for problem-solving. Avoid using the Northwest Small Tai Ji to place your bed. The North Small Tai Ji would be a better option. When seeing water externally, the occupants of this room tend to become overly emotional and sometimes easily depressed.

The South sector can also make a favorable bedroom. Occupants here will experience general good health and well being. When the size of the room includes both the South and Southeast sectors, the combined effect is auspicious for education and learning, writing and designing as well as property development. Alternately using the Southeast Small Tai Ji of a South sector room will have similar positive effects. When supported externally by a hill or mountain, then the occupants will also be blessed with long life. Gua #6 and #7 persons using this room will not receive this extra benefits though.

The North sector can be used as a temporary bedroom, but losses its effectiveness as we approach Period 9.

Southwest 1 (未) Facing Homes in Period 8

Where do you put your bed?

Best Location	Northeast
2ⁿᵈ Best Location	Northwest
3ʳᵈ Best Location	West
4ᵗʰ Best Location	South

Commentary

The Period 8 Southwest 1 facing property has FOUR positive bedroom sectors! The most powerful bedroom would be the Northeast sector. Aside from overall good health, this room also enhances the property luck of its occupants. When supported externally by hill or mountain, there would be immense wealth as a result from wise property investments. This room is also usable for those seeking rest and retirement.

The second best bedroom is the Northwest sector. The Literary Formation enhances intelligence, reputation, and recognition. This room also connects you with important people who can help improve your life. If this is your room, you must capitalize on your connections. Gua #6 persons benefits the most from using this bedroom. Aside from the Southwest Small Tai Ji, all other locations are acceptable for bed placement in this room.

The West sector contains the Future Prosperous Star #9. this of course promotes good health and relationships. Persons using this room will excel in creative or right-brained careers such as movie directors, abstract painters and all designers. Interestingly, this room also improves self-esteem.

The South sector has a special formation called 'Oyster Revealing its Pearl', especially when supported by a Metal shaped hill externally. The occupants of this room will be exceptionally talented in various fields, whether in academics, business or beauty. This room is highly beneficial for females. Males using this room will do very well in female dominated businesses such as jewelry, lingerie, and beauty products. Avoid using the Southwest or Northeast Small Tai Ji, as they counter the effects of the special formation.

Southwest 2 (坤) or Southwest 3 (申) Facing Homes in Period 8

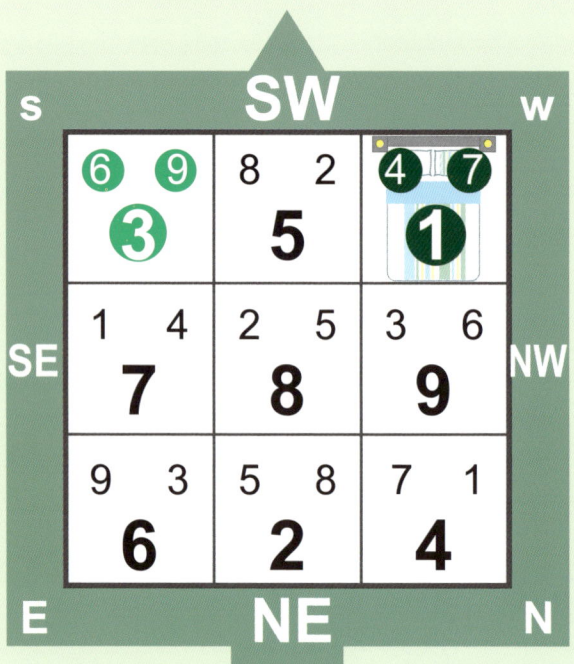

Where do you put your bed?

Best Location	West
2nd Best Location	South

Commentary

For a Period 8 Southwest 2 / 3 facing property, the West sector can be considered a positive room. When supported by external higher ground, this room promotes health and networking. Occupants of this room will be very well connected with the right people when using the Southeast Small Tai Ji. If there is an open field outside the West sector, wealth opportunities will present itself through niche services and markets. In other words, you will be rewarded for being different from the rest in your chosen industry. When afflicted by negative external forms, be vary of scandals, frauds and being conned.

The South sector should also be supported externally by a hill or higher ground. Failing which the occupants of this room will experience migraine, poor memory and feet injuries. When properly supported, this room promises great power and demands wide spread respect. Gua #6 and #7 persons are disadvantaged if using this bedroom. The bed must be placed at Southeast or Southwest Small Tai Ji locations to benefits from the positive effects of the bedroom.

The Seating Star #8 in the Southwest palace is rendered useless due to its violation of the Direct & Indirect Spirit principal.

West 1 (庚) Facing Homes in Period 8

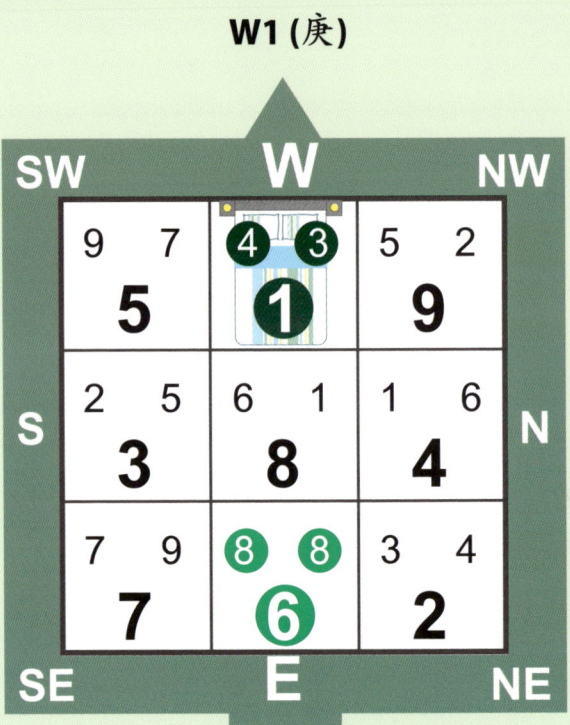

Where do you put your bed?

Best Location	West
2nd Best Location	East

Your Head Here

Commentary

The Period 8 West 1 facing property is considered one of the special conditions chart of all 16 Flying Stars chart. The West sector can be used under two circumstances. As an individual room, the #4 Green star is considered unstable. When supported by external hills, this star makes excellent business people, corporate climbers and skilled strategists. However, even in its positive form the health aspect is just average for the occupants of this room.

The #4 Green star can be brought to its prosperous level when used in conjunction with the Southwest. That is to say the West and Southwest sectors should be combined as one entire room. Then, this room will support good health and relationships, as well as power and authority. Whatever physical illness that thus occur can be solved with surgery.

Here is another trade secret: using the Southwest Small Tai Ji of the West sector room will also simulate the above effects.

The next available bedroom would be the East sector. However, East should also be combined with Northeast sector. When supported externally by a Wood shaped mountain or building, this room enhances positive health and prolongs lifespan, and the occupants will gain good reputation and respect for their contribution in their chosen fields. This configuration is most suitable for Gua #1 and Gua #4 persons, and less suitable for Gua #2 persons.

Note that the prosperous Sitting Star #8 in the East sector is redundant when used in isolation, as it violates the principal of Direct and Indirect spirit.

West 2 (酉) or West 3 (辛) Facing Homes in Period 8

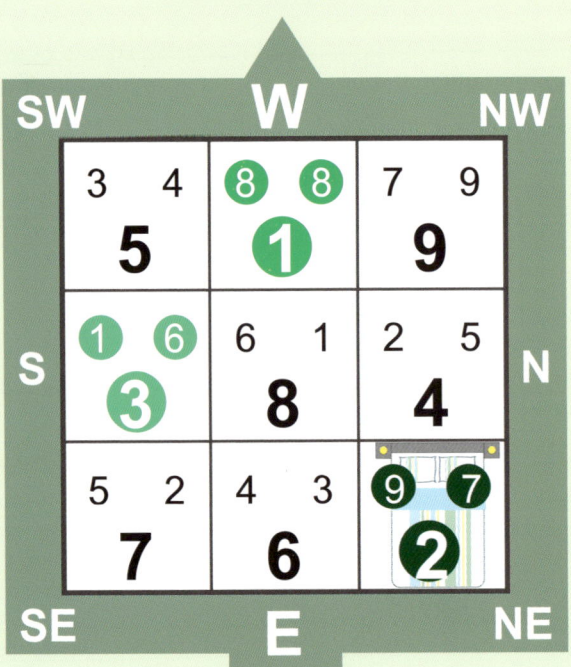

Where do you put your bed?

Best Location	Northeast
2nd Best Location	West
3rd Best Location	South

Your Head Here

Commentary

For this house, the Northeast sector is extremely beneficial, due to the presence of the Future Prosperous Star #9. This star promotes good health and fulfilling relationships. The bed should be ideally located in the East Small Tai Ji of this bedroom.

The West sector is also a good room to use with the presence of the Prosperous Seating Star #8. In this configuration, the #8 star should not be used in conjunction with Southwest. This means your bed should not be in the Southwest Small Tai Ji. Use the South Small Tai Ji instead. This room promotes good health and overall stability.

The South sector is also considered a positive room, as the stars here enhance health, intelligence, recognition, and business acumen. Use the East Small Tai Ji of this room for maximum positive effects.

Northwest 1 (戌) Facing Homes in Period 8

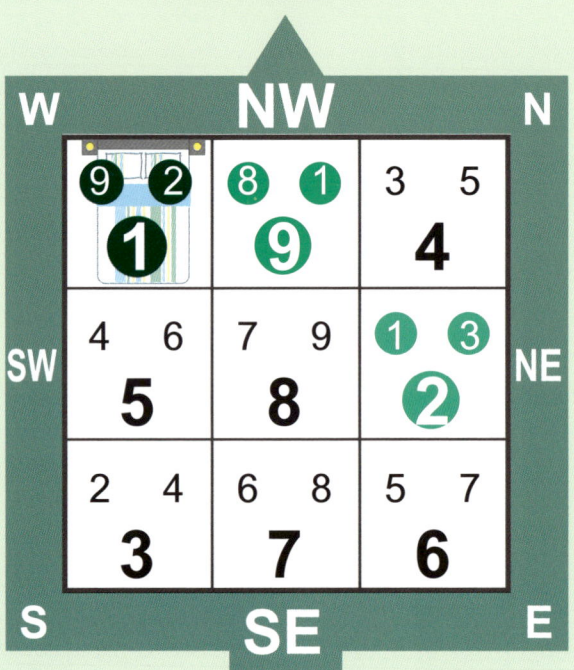

Where do you put your bed?

Best Location	West
2nd Best Location	Northwest
3rd Best Location	Northeast

Commentary

The Northwest 1 facing house has three positive bedrooms – the West sector being the best of the lot. Using this room not only enhances your physical health and emotional well being, but also makes you look more attractive! Of course, when the externals are afflicted by negative water forms, then reverse is true. Those who are in the beauty business, PR and communications, bridal and wedding, as well as entertainment and advertising can benefit from the stars in this sector. All Small Tai Ji locations are usable for bed placement in this room.

The second best room in this house is the Northwest sector. This room is all about stability, balance, and self-cultivation. The positive effect of this room tends to grow with time, and is a suitable room for everyone. The best Small Tai Ji location to place your bed would be the West, but otherwise all other locations are generally acceptable too.

The Northeast sector is a positive room, especially for younger till middle aged persons. This is because the 1-3 combination is vibrant and active, promising lots of travel and meeting people. As such those in sales and marketing, hotel and tourism, or even research and development – will do very well when using this bedroom. If there is a hill outside the Northeast sector, then recognition and Noble help comes eve faster! Placing your bed on exactly Northeast 3 of the 24 Mountains will bring fastest results, especially for those born in the year of the Horse or Pig.

Your Head Here

Northwest 2 (乾) or Northwest 3 (亥) Facing Homes in Period 8

Where do you put your bed?

Best Location	Northwest
2nd Best Location	Northeast

Commentary

The first available sector for this house is the Northwest sector. The Sitting Star #6 here is strong and supported, presenting good health and lasting endurance to its occupants. Overall this sector represents authority, fair governance and leadership qualities. Those in managerial positions, judicial systems, and roles that require fast executions will do well. Within this room use the Southwest Small Tai Ji or the North Small Tai Ji to place your bed.

The Northeast sector is also considered a positive bedroom, even though the good qualities are considered average. When not afflicted by Sha Qi, this room promotes scholarly and military achievements. Therefore, writers, researchers, educators as well as sportsmen and martial artists will fare well in this bedroom.

North 1 (壬) Facing Homes in Period 8

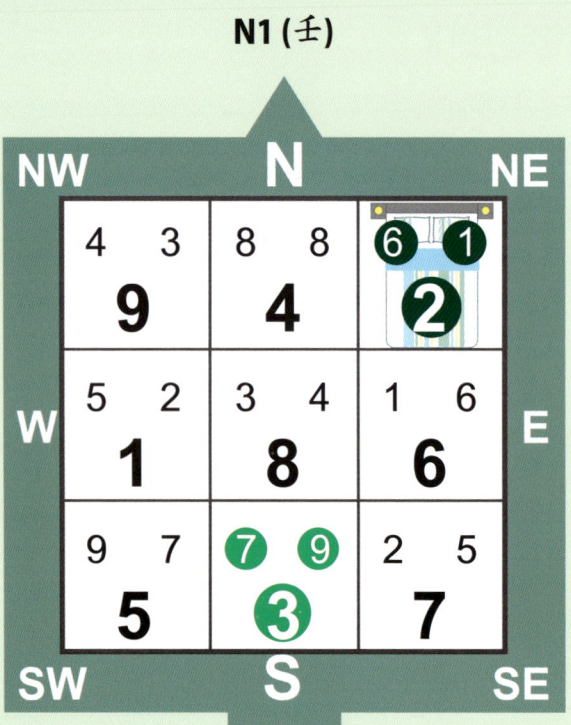

Where do you put your bed?

Best Location	Northeast
2nd Best Location	South

Commentary

For a Period 8 North 1 facing property, the first choice bedroom is in the Northeast sector. The stars here support health and vitality, as well as understanding and communication in relationships. When supported by external forms, this room produces powerful people and well-connected businessmen. Place your bed in the North Small Tai Ji or the East Small Tai Ji for maximum results.

The South sector can also make an auspicious bedroom, provided that it is connected to the Southeast. Under this condition, this room enhances positive feelings and creative inspirations. Those in the IT field, advertising and broadcasting, performing arts, as well as F&B will do extremely well under the special conditions of this room. If matched with positive forms, the effects from this room will be magnified.

In the occasion that the South sector is a stand alone room, ensure that the bed is located in the Southeast Small Tai Ji. This room is better suited for Gua #2 and Gua #8 people.

North 2 (子) or North 3 (癸) Facing Homes in Period 8

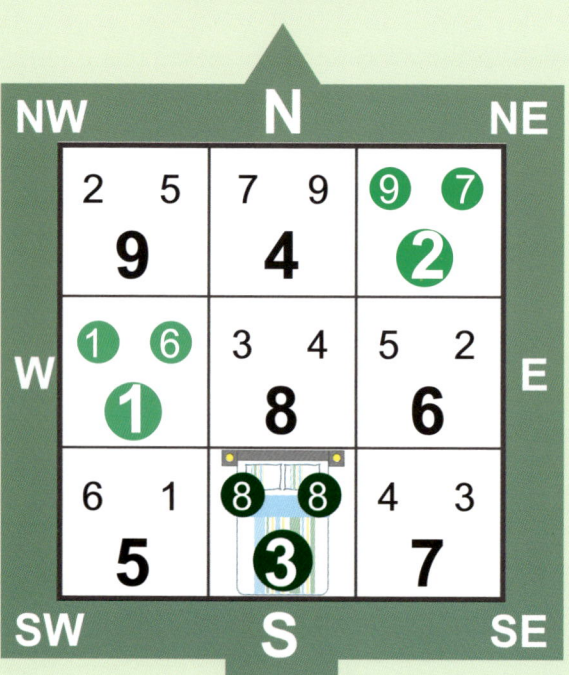

Where do you put your bed?

Best Location	South
2nd Best Location	Northeast
3rd Best Location	West

Commentary

The South sector room is extremely stable for this North 2 / 3 facing property. Not only will the occupants be healthy and happy, they will also seek to constantly improve themselves. Creative talents will also meet opportunities to become financially profitable when using this bedroom. Locate your bed in the West Small Tai Ji for maximum results.

The Northeast sector is also a very stable room, promising good health and constant motivation. Work that involves influencing others or inspiring faith will do well under the influence of this sector. In its negative form, this room causes paranoia, obsessive behavior, and constant rage to its occupants. This can occur when the shape of the room is uneven.

The West sector is basically a very positive room to sleep in, but for the North 3 facing house specifically, the stars in this room becomes a special formation called the 'Full Moon Rising over the Ocean'. This formation is especially beneficial for females, bringing power and wealth from behind the scenes. When not afflicted by any negative features, this room produces charismatic and highly intelligent people.

Northeast 1 (丑) Facing Homes in Period 8

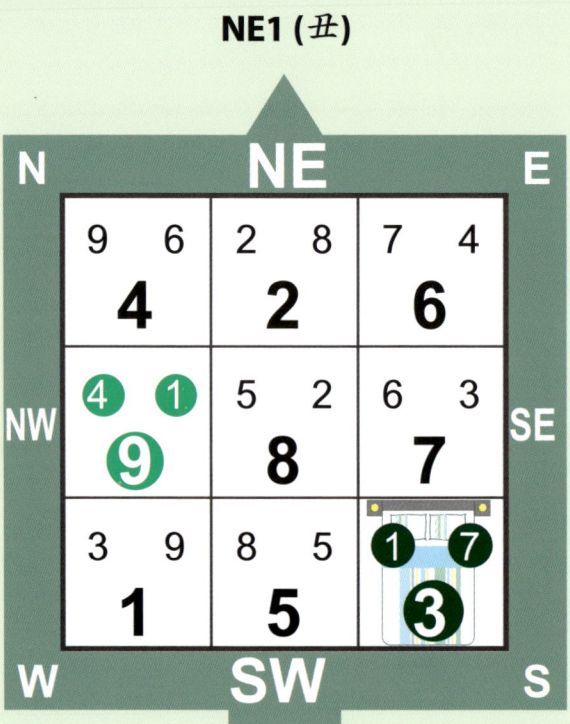

Where do you put your bed?

Best Location	South
2nd Best Location	Northwest

Commentary

The Period 8 Northeast 1 facing house has its best bedroom in the South sector. The stars here support health and relationships. Those whose work involves speaking will fare well by using this room. Generally, occupants of this room will receive wealth from females, and therefore businesses that involve a female market will flourish.

The Northwest sector contains the Literary Formation. So those involved in education, writing, creative arts, and research will be supported by this bedroom. All Small Tai Ji locations in this room are generally is acceptable for bed placement. When supported by external hills this room promises fame and fortune.

Additionally the Northeast sector can be used as a bedroom, so long as it is combined with either the North or East sectors respectively. Using this sector brings long term property luck to the occupants.

Northeast 2 (艮) or Northeast 3 (寅) Facing Homes in Period 8

Where do you put your bed?

Best Location	Northeast
2nd Best Location	Northwest
3rd Best Location	South

Commentary

For this property, the Northeast sector is an extremely stable bedroom location. The stars here promote rest, rejuvenation, and health at all levels. The only possible drawback is that married couples might find their passion and excitement dwindling with time. That aside, this is still a very positive bedroom, where all Small Tai Ji locations can be used to place your bed. If there is a hill or mountain outside the Northeast, one will be able to leave a legacy behind or contribute to society in a large scale manner.

The Northwest sector is the perfect bedroom for project managers, team leaders, and sales directors. Work that involves planning and quick execution is supported by this room. For maximum effect, place the bed in the North Small Tai Ji. This room is not suitable for Gua #3 people.

The Future Prosperous Star #9 in the South sector enhances good mood and self confidence. Aside from good health, this room also promotes beauty and fame especially when supported by external higher ground. This sector is not suitable however for male children generally. They tend to be rebel against authority and the father. The bed should be placed at the Southeast Small Tai Ji ideally. If you have no choice but to place your male child in this room, then use the Southwest sub-sector for his bed location.

Your Head Here

East 1 (甲) Facing Homes in Period 8

Where do you put your bed?

Best Location	Northeast
2nd Best Location	West

Commentary

The Period 8 East 1 facing chart has two positive bedroom locations but they are not considered as superior palaces.

Firstly the Northeast sector is viable for its gentle and soothing nature. The stars here improve health through rest and relaxation as well as supplements and vitamins. If there is a busy road or fast moving water outside here, this room causes stress and anxiety to its occupants. When conditions are positive, this room also promotes literary excellence and success in painting, drawing or dancing. Within this room the East Small Tai Ji and the North Small Tai Ji are considered ideal bed locations.

West sector is considered a positive bedroom only if there is higher ground outside. When this Feng Shui requirement is met, then this room brings leadership and charisma. This bedroom is also suitable for performers, singers, and stuntmen. Public speakers will also benefit by using this room. When matched specifically by a Metal shaped mountain externally, this becomes the 'Thunder in the Western Skies' – bringing sudden fame, respect and power to its occupants.

Your Head Here

East 2 (卯) or East 3 (乙) Facing Homes in Period 8

Where do you put your bed?

Best Location	West
2nd Best Location	Northwest
3rd Best Location	Northeast

Commentary

For a Period 8 East 2 / 3 facing property, the West sector is the most stable bedroom. Hence, it promotes long term health and balance at all levels – physically, mentally and emotionally. Using this room also allows residual income and financial gains from behind the scenes. This room is suitable for people of all Gua. Your bed can be placed at any Small Tai Ji locations within this room.

The Future Prosperous Star #9 in the Northwest brings good health, happiness and a general sense of fulfillment. This room is suitable for those in the IT business, oil and gas, electronics, and spirituality. This room is less beneficial for Gua #7 persons. The bed should ideally be placed in the West Small Tai Ji.

Specifically for the East 3 facing house, the Northeast sector is a special bedroom with the formation 'A Jewel Rising from the Ground'. The bed should be located in the Northeast 1 sector of the 24 Mountains, as measured from the centre of the property. This formation produces extremely talented and elegant individuals. Normally they become business strategists or advisors to large corporate entities. Using this room gives you influence by means of intelligence and unconventional tactics. Ideally of course, the Northeast external should see a hill or higher ground.

Your Head Here

Southeast 1 (辰) Facing Homes in Period 8

Where do you put your bed?

Best Location	Northwest
2nd Best Location	South
3rd Best Location	Northeast

Commentary

The Period 8 Southeast 1 facing property has one superior bedroom location and two average bedroom locations.

The Northwest sector contains a host of special stars – making this room balanced in terms of health, wealth, and relationships. This room is a especially beneficial for males. Those running their own business should sleep in this sector. For the exact bed location, avoid the West and North Small Tai Ji respectively. When supported by external natural hills, this sector brings in multiple sources of indirect wealth.

The South sector is also acceptable to be used as a bedroom. This sector is good for academic scholars, translators, writers, bloggers, and those in the creative arts. When afflicted by negative features externally, the occupants of this room will experience migraine, wind problems and gastric. When positively supported, this room enhances ones good name and brings it to foreign land. Within this room, place your bed in the Southwest Small Tai Ji.

The Northeast sector room is suitable for middle aged people pursuing a fast moving career. Those involved in sales and travelling will do well when using this room. The bed can be placed in the Southeast Small Tai Ji in the Northwest. If the room door opens at the West Small Tai Ji of the room, this denotes recognition and excellence for the occupants.

Southeast 2 (巽) or Southeast 3 (巳) Facing Homes in Period 8

Where do you put your bed?

Best Location	Northwest
2nd Best Location	Northeast

Commentary

For a Period 8 Southeast 2 / 3 facing house, the most stable bedroom would be in the Northwest sector. This room promotes overall good health and calmness. Those working for others will find their careers generally smooth-sailing when sleeping in this bedroom. When supported by higher ground behind, the occupants will be respected for their humility and balanced approach to life. The bed should be located in the Northeast Small Tai Ji, and it's suitable to be used by individuals of any Gua.

The Northeast sector is another favorable bedroom location. This sector improves overall health, especially for those interested in body building. Physical trainers, massage therapists, and sportsmen will perform better under the influence of this room. Do note however that the main star of this sector is not compatible with Gua #3 occupants. The most ideal location for the bed is the Southeast Small Tai Ji.

Additionally, all remaining sectors are considered as average grade bedrooms and are therefore usable. The South sector is considered the most negative bedroom for this house – the Sitting Star #5 is extremely volatile here.

6

Chapter 7:
Bedroom (Feng Shui) Secrets

Bedroom (Feng Shui) Secrets

Now that you have decided where the positive bedroom sectors are – what next?

If you are moving into a new house, then it is easy. Just decide to use the most positive sector (or at least, one of the good sectors prescribed) as your bedroom. If the exact location of the bed is not stipulated, then any sub-sector within that room would be fine. Just be mindful of the Bed Rules in Chapter 2.

In the rare occasion where all the recommended rooms are not available, or there are no good sectors for you to sleep in – then look for higher ground. Like I have mentioned before, mountains support the bed's Yin-strength, so look for where the mountain is. If you do not see a mountain, then look for hills, or higher ground – these constitutes as your stability factor from the external.

If you cannot determine which side of the road is higher, here's a 'secret': wait for it to rain, then see which way the water flows. Because water always follows gravity, moving from higher ground, to lower ground. Never, ever assume that higher ground is where most traffic comes from (don't laugh, I've been asked this before)

For those of you who are more well-versed in Feng Shui, especially with the Life Gua personal directions, can opt to combine this knowledge with the prescribed room locations. For example, if your favorable direction is

Southeast, then you can position your headboard to face Southeast. This is, however, NOT the most crucial part of your bedroom Feng Shui. What is more important is getting IN to the right room first.

When all else fails, or if things become too complicated for you, then you the safest option to get your Feng Shui done is to get the help of a qualified Feng Shui practitioner.

Move Your Bed on an Auspicious Date

Once you have decided you want to move your bed into a different, better location, and select a good date for this. This is important even if you want to only move sub-sectors within the same room.

- Select a Success or Open Day if you are using the 12 Officers system. Make sure that the Branch of the Day does not clash with the Branch of your Year Pillar in your BaZi. So for example, if you are born in the year of the Snake, do not select a Pig Day that is also a Success or Open Day.

For those with some knowledge of Date Selection or who have read Joey Yap's book *The Art of Date Selection: Personal Date Selection*, you can take it a step further.

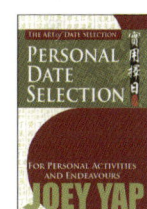

- Select a Success or Open Day according to the 12 Officers system. Ensure the Branch of the Day does not clash your Year Pillar Branch.
- The Success or Open Day should contain your Wealth Element, as dictated by your BaZi, on the Stem. This will ensure that installing the aquarium on that date does bring wealth.
- Use only Success or Open Days which satisfy the above criteria, which are also Superior Days, according to the Dong Gong System.

7

Bedroom (Feng Shui) Secrets

MASTERY ACADEMY
OF CHINESE METAPHYSICS

Your **Preferred** Choice to the Art & Science of Classical Chinese Metaphysics Studies

Bringing **innovative** techniques and **creative** teaching methods to an ancient study.

Mastery Academy of Chinese Metaphysics was established by Joey Yap to play the role of disseminating this Eastern knowledge to the modern world with the belief that this valuable knowledge should be accessible to anyone, anywhere.

Its goal is to enrich people's lives through accurate, professional teaching and practice of Chinese Metaphysics knowledge globally. It is the first academic institution of its kind in the world to adopt the tradition of Western institutions of higher learning - where students are encourage to explore, question and challenge themselves and to respect different fields and branches of study - with the appreciation and respect of classical ideas and applications that have stood the test of time.

The art and science of Chinese Metaphysics studies – be it Feng Shui, BaZi (Astrology), Mian Xiang (Face Reading), ZeRi (Date Selection) or Yi Jing – is no longer a field shrouded with mystery and superstition. In light of new technology, fresher interpretations and innovative methods as well as modern teaching tools like the Internet, interactive learning, e-learning and distance learning, anyone from virtually any corner of the globe, who is keen to master these disciplines can do so with ease and confidence under the guidance and support of the Academy.

It has indeed proven to be a center of educational excellence for thousands of students from over thirty countries across the world; many of whom have moved on to practice classical Chinese Metaphysics professionally in their home countries.

At the Academy, we believe in enriching people's lives by empowering their destinies through the disciplines of Chinese Metaphysics. Learning is not an option - it's a way of life!

MASTERY ACADEMY
OF CHINESE METAPHYSICS™

MALAYSIA
19-3, The Boulevard, Mid Valley City, 59200 Kuala Lumpur, Malaysia
Tel : +603-2284 8080 | Fax : +603-2284 1218
Email   : info@masteryacademy.com
Website : www.masteryacademy.com

Australia, Austria, Canada, China, Croatia, Cyprus, Czech Republic, Denmark, France, Germany, Greece, Hungary, India, Italy, Kazakhstan, Malaysia, Netherlands (Holland), New Zealand, Philippines, Poland, Russian Federation, Singapore, Slovenia, South Africa, Switzerland, Turkey, U.S.A., Ukraine, United Kingdom

www.masteryacademy.com | +603 - 2284 8080

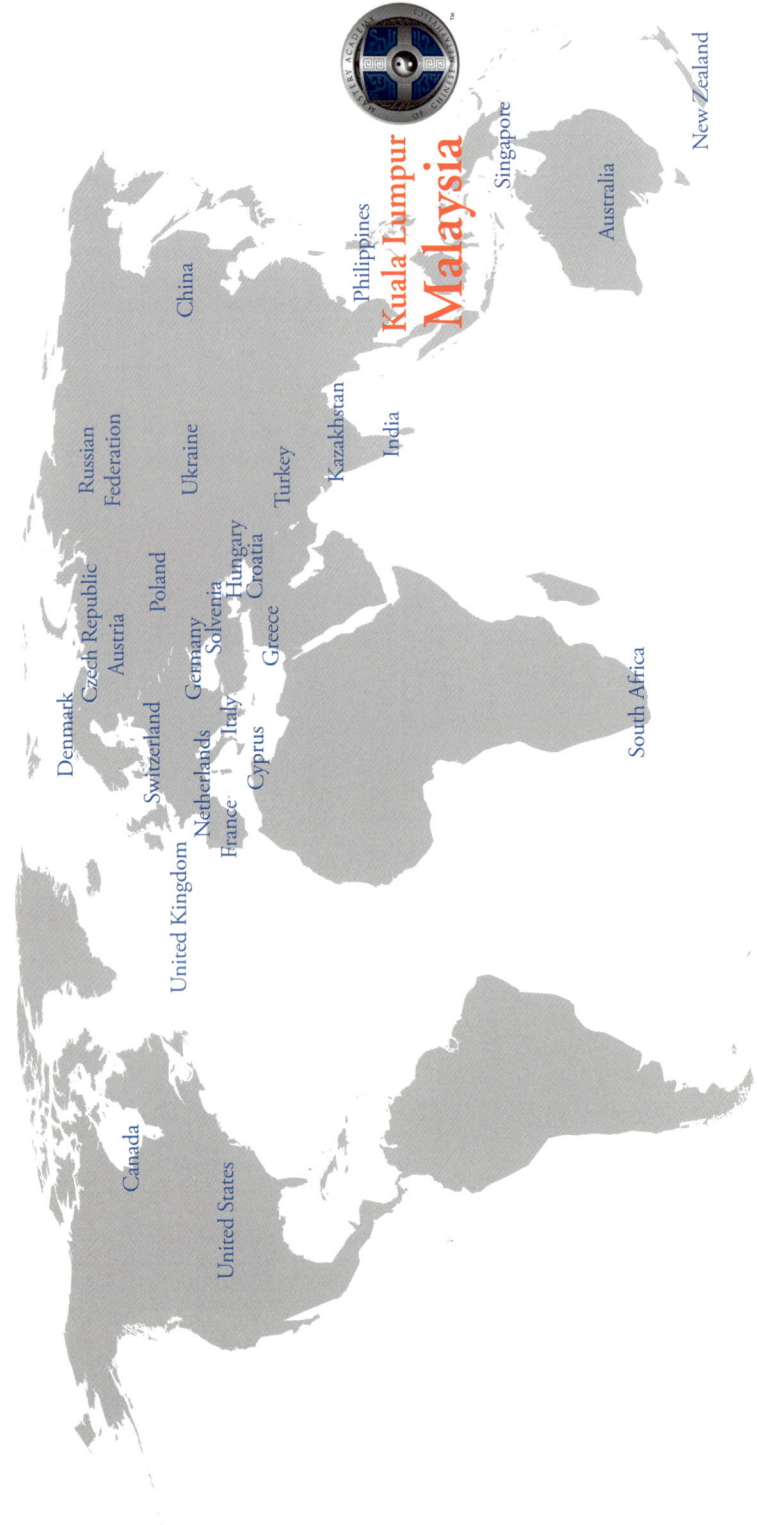

JOEY YAP CONSULTING GROUP

Pioneering Metaphysics - Centric Personal Coaching and Corporate Consulting

The Joey Yap Consulting Group is the world's first specialised metaphysics consultation firm. Founded in 2002 by renown international Feng Shui and BaZi consultant, author and trainer Joey Yap, the Joey Yap Consulting Group is a pioneer in the provision of metaphysics-driven coaching and consultation services for individuals and corporations.

The Group's core consultation practice areas are Feng Shui and BaZi, which are complimented by ancillary services like Date Selection, Face Reading and Yi Jing Divination. The Group's team of highly-trained professional consultants are led by Principal Consultant Joey Yap. The Joey Yap Consulting Group is the firm of choice for corporate captains, entrepreneurs, celebrities and property developers when it comes to Feng Shui and BaZi-related advisory and knowledge.

Across Industries: Our Portfolio of Clients

Our diverse portfolio of both corporate and individual clients from all around the world bears testimony to our experience and capabilities.

Joey Yap Consulting Group is the firm of choice for many of Asia's leading multi-national corporations, listed entities, conglomerates and top-tier property developers when it comes to Feng Shui and corporate BaZi.

Our services also engaged by professionals, prominent business personalities, celebrities, high-profile politicians and people from all walks of life.

JOEY YAP CONSULTING GROUP

Name (Mr./Mrs./Ms.):_____

Contact Details

Tel:_____ Fax:_____

Mobile :_____

Email:_____

What Type of Consultation Are You Interested In?
☐ Feng Shui ☐ BaZi ☐ Date Selection ☐ Corporate Events

Please tick if applicable:
☐ Are you a Property Developer looking to engage Joey Yap Consulting Group?
☐ Are you a Property Investor looking for tailor-made packages to suit your investment requirements?

Please attach your name card here.

Thank you for completing this form. Please fax it back to us at:

Malaysia & the rest of the world
Fax : +603-2284 2213   Tel : +603-2284 1213

www.joeyyap.com

Feng Shui Consultations

For Residential Properties
- Initial Land/Property Assessment
- Residential Feng Shui Consultations
- Residential Land Selection
- End-to-End Residential Consultation

For Commercial Properties
- Initial Land/Property Assessment
- Commercial Feng Shui Consultations
- Commercial Land Selection
- End-to-End Commercial Consultation

For Property Developers
- End-to-End Consultation
- Post-Consultation Advisory Services
- Panel Feng Shui Consultant

For Property Investors
- Your Personal Feng Shui Consultant
- Tailor-Made Packages

For Memorial Parks & Burial Sites
- Yin House Feng Shui

BaZi Consultations

Personal Destiny Analysis
- Personal Destiny Analysis for Individuals
- Children's BaZi Analysis
- Family BaZi Analysis

Strategic Analysis for Corporate Organizations
- Corporate BaZi Consultations
- BaZi Analysis for Human Resource Management

Entrepreneurs & Business Owners
- BaZi Analysis for Entrepreneurs

Career Pursuits
- BaZi Career Analysis

Relationships
- Marriage and Compatibility Analysis
- Partnership Analysis

For Everyone
- Annual BaZi Forecast
- Your Personal BaZi Coach

Date Selection Consultations

- Marriage Date Selection
- Caesarean Birth Date Selection
- House-Moving Date Selection
- Renovation & Groundbreaking Dates
- Signing of Contracts
- Official Openings
- Product Launches

Corporate Events

Many reputable organizations and instituitions have worked closely with Joey Yap Consulting Group to build a synergistic business relationship by engaging our team of consultants, led by Joey Yap, as speakers at their corporate events.

We tailor our seminars and talks to suit the anticipated or pertinent group of audience. Be it department, subsidiary, your clients or even the entire corporation, we aim to fit your requirements in delivering the intended message(s).

Tel: +603-2284 1213   Email: consultation@joeyyap.com

CHINESE METAPHYSICS REFERENCE SERIES

The Chinese Metaphysics Reference Series is a collection of reference texts, source material, and educational textbooks to be used as supplementary guides by scholars, students, researchers, teachers and practitioners of Chinese Metaphysics.

These comprehensive and structured books provide fast, easy reference to aid in the study and practice of various Chinese Metaphysics subjects including Feng Shui, BaZi, Yi Jing, Zi Wei, Liu Ren, Ze Ri, Ta Yi, Qi Men and Mian Xiang.

The Chinese Metaphysics Compendium

At over 1,000 pages, the *Chinese Metaphysics Compendium* is a unique one-volume reference book that compiles all the formulas relating to Feng Shui, BaZi (Four Pillars of Destiny), Zi Wei (Purple Star Astrology), Yi Jing (I-Ching), Qi Men (Mystical Doorways), Ze Ri (Date Selection), Mian Xiang (Face Reading) and other sources of Chinese Metaphysics.

It is presented in the form of easy-to-read tables, diagrams and reference charts, all of which are compiled into one handy book. This first-of-its-kind compendium is presented in both English and the original Chinese, so that none of the meanings and contexts of the technical terminologies are lost.

The only essential and comprehensive reference on Chinese Metaphysics, and an absolute must-have for all students, scholars, and practitioners of Chinese Metaphysics.

The Ten Thousand Year Calendar (Pocket Edition)

The Ten Thousand Year Calendar

Dong Gong Date Selection

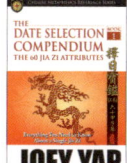
The Date Selection Compendium

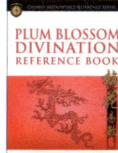
Plum Blossoms Divination Reference Book

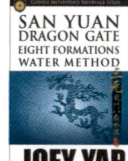
San Yuan Dragon Gate Eight Formations Water Method

Xuan Kong Da Gua Ten Thousand Year Calendar

Bazi Hour Pillar Useful Gods - Wood

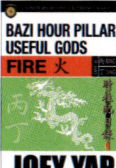
Bazi Hour Pillar Useful Gods - Fire

Bazi Hour Pillar Useful Gods - Earth

Bazi Hour Pillar Useful Gods - Metal

Bazi Hour Pillar Useful Gods - Water

Xuan Kong Da Gua Structures Reference Book

Xuan Kong Da Gua 64 Gua Transformation Analysis

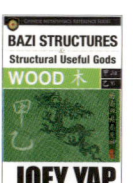
Bazi Structures and Structural Useful Gods - Wood

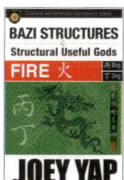
Bazi Structures and Structural Useful Gods - Fire

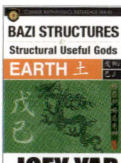
Bazi Structures and Structural Useful Gods - Earth

Bazi Structures and Structural Useful Gods - Metal

Bazi Structures and Structural Useful Gods - Water

Xuan Kong Purple White Script

Earth Study Discern Truth Second Edition

www.masteryacademy.com | +603 - 2284 8080

Joey Yap's BaZi Profiling System

Three Levels of BaZi Profiling (English & Chinese versions)

In BaZi Profiling, there are three levels that reflect three different stages of a person's personal nature and character structure.

Level 1 – The Day Master

The Day Master in a nutshell is the BASIC YOU. The inborn personality. It is your essential character. It answers the basic question "WHO AM I". There are ten basic personality profiles – the TEN Day Masters – each with its unique set of personality traits, likes and dislikes.

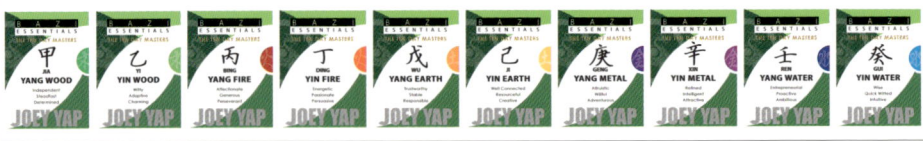

Level 2 – The Structure

The Structure is your behavior and attitude – in other words, how you use your personality. It expands on the Day Master (Level 1). The structure reveals your natural tendencies in life – are you more controlling, more of a creator, supporter, thinker or connector? Each of the Ten Day Masters express themselves differently through the FIVE Structures. Why do we do the things we do? Why do we like the things we like? – The answers are in our BaZi STRUCTURE.

Level 3 – The Profile

The Profile reveals your unique abilities and skills, the masks that you consciously and unconsciously "put on" as you approach and navigate the world. Your Profile speaks of your ROLES in life. There are TEN roles – or Ten BaZi Profiles. Everyone plays a different role.

What makes you happy and what does success mean to you is different to somebody else. Your sense of achievement and sense of purpose in life is unique to your Profile. Your Profile will reveal your unique style.

The path of least resistance to your success and wealth can only be accessed once you get into your "flow." Your BaZi Profile reveals how you can get FLOW. It will show you your patterns in work, relationship and social settings. Being AWARE of these patterns is your first step to positive Life Transformation.

www.baziprofiling.com

BaZi Collections

Leading Chinese Astrology Master Trainer Joey Yap makes it easy to learn how to unlock your Destiny through your BaZi with these books. BaZi or Four Pillars of Destiny is an ancient Chinese science which enables individuals to understand their personality, hidden talents and abilities as well as their luck cycle, simply by examining the information contained within their birth data.

Understand and appreciate more about this astoundingly accurate ancient Chinese Metaphysical science with this BaZi Collection.

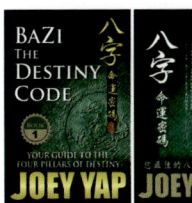  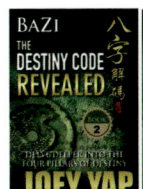  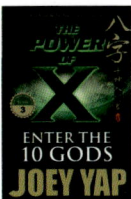 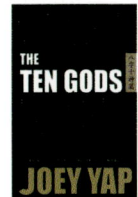

Feng Shui Collection

Must-Haves for Property Analysis!

For homeowners, those looking to build their own home or even investors who are looking to apply Feng Shui to their homes, these series of books provides valuable information from the classical Feng Shui therioes and applications.

In his trademark straight-to-the-point manner, Joey shares with you the Feng Shui do's and dont's when it comes to finding a property with favorable Feng Shui, which is condusive for home living.

  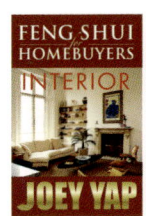  

Stories & Lessons on Feng Shui Series

All in all, this series is a delightful chronicle of Joey's articles, thoughts and vast experience - as a professional Feng Shui consultant and instructor - that have been purposely refined, edited and expanded upon to make for a light-hearted, interesting yet educational read. And with Feng Shui, BaZi, Mian Xiang and Yi Jing all thrown into this one dish, there's something for everyone.

 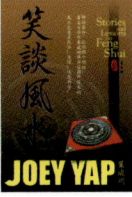  

www.masteryacademy.com | +603 - 2284 8080

Continue Your Journey with Joey Yap Books in Feng Shui

Pure Feng Shui
Pure Feng Shui is Joey Yap's debut with an international publisher, CICO Books, and is a refreshing and elegant look at the intricacies of Classical Feng Shui – now compiled in a useful manner for modern-day readers. This book is a comprehensive introduction to all the important precepts and techniques of Feng Shui practice.

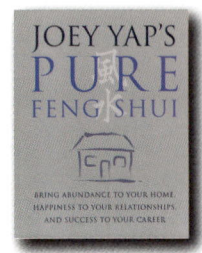

Your Aquarium Here
This book is the first in Fengshuilogy Series, a series of matter-in-fact and useful Feng Shui books designed for the person who wants to do a fuss-free Feng Shui.

Xuan Kong Flying Stars
This book is an essential introductory book to the subject of Xuan Kong Fei Xing, a well-known and popular system of Feng Shui. Learn 'tricks of the trade' and 'trade secrets' to enhance and maximize Qi in your home or office.

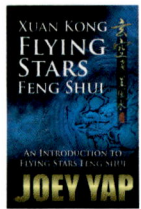

Walking the Dragons
Compiled in one book for the first time from Joey Yap's Feng Shui Mastery Excursion Series, the book highlights China's extensive, vibrant history with astute observations on the Feng Shui of important sites and places. Learn the landform formations of Yin Houses (tombs and burial places), as well as mountains, temples, castles, and villages.

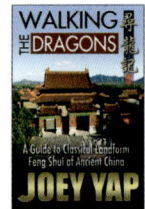

The Art of Date Selection: Personal Date Selection
With the *Art of Date Selection: Personal Date Selection*, learn simple, practical methods you can employ to select not just good dates, but personalized good dates. Whether it's a personal activity such as a marriage or professional endeavor such as launching a business, signing a contract or even acquiring assets, this book will show you how to pick the good dates and tailor them to suit the activity in question, as well as avoid the negative ones too!

www.masteryacademy.com | +603 - 2284 8080

Face Reading Collection

Discover Face Reding (English & Chinese versions)

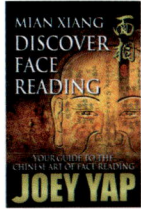 

This is a comprehensive book on all areas of Face Reading, covering some of the most important facial features, including the forehead, mouth, ears and even philtrum above your lips. This book eill help you analyse not just your Destiny but help you achieve your full potential and achieve life fulfillment.

Joey Yap's Art of Face Reading

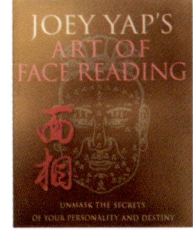

The Art of Face Reading is Joey Yap's second effort with CICO Books, and takes a lighter, more practical approach to Face Reading. This book does not so much focus on the individual features as it does on reading the entire face. It is about identifying common personality types and characters.

Easy Guide on Face Reading (English & Chinese versions)

The Face Reading Essentials series of books comprises 5 individual books on the key features of the face – Eyes, Eyebrows, Ears, Nose, and Mouth. Each book provides a detailed illustration and a simple yet descriptive explanation on the individual types of the features.

The books are equally useful and effective for beginners, enthusiasts, and the curious. The series is designed to enable people who are new to Face Reading to make the most of first impressions and learn to apply Face Reading skills to understand the personality and character of friends, family, co-workers, and even business associates.

  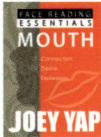  

Annual Releases

2011 Annual Outlook & Tong Shu

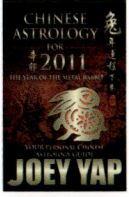 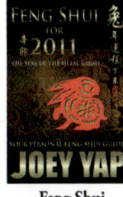  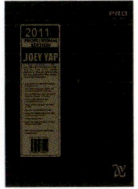  

Chinese Astrology for 2011 | Feng Shui for 2011 | Tong Shu Desktop Calendar 2011 | Professional Tong Shu Diary 2011 | Tong Shu Monthly Planner 2011 | Weekly Tong Shu Diary 2011

www.masteryacademy.com | +603 - 2284 8080

Educational Tools and Software

Xuan Kong Flying Stars Feng Shui Software
The Essential Application for Enthusiasts and Professionals

The Xuan Kong Flying Stars Feng Shui Software will assist you in the practice of Xuan Kong Feng Shui with minimum fuss and maximum effectiveness. Superimpose the Flying Stars charts over your house plans (or those of your clients) to clearly demarcate the 9 Palaces. Use it to help you create fast and sophisticated chart drawings and presentations, as well as to assist professional practitioners in the report-writing process before presenting the final reports for your clients. Students can use it to practice their Xuan Kong Feng Shui skills and knowledge, and it can even be used by designers and architects!

BaZi Ming Pan Software Version 2.0
Professional Four Pillars Calculator for Destiny Analysis

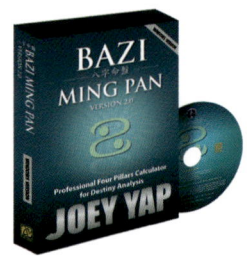

The BaZi Ming Pan Version 2.0 Professional Four Pillars Calculator for Destiny Analysis is the most technically advanced software of its kind in the world today. It allows even those without any knowledge of BaZi to generate their own BaZi Charts, and provides virtually every detail required to undertake a comprehensive Destiny Analysis.

This Professional Four Pillars Calculator allows you to even undertake a day-to-day analysis of your Destiny. What's more, all BaZi Charts generated by this software are fully printable and configurable! Designed for both enthusiasts and professional practitioners, this state-of-the-art software blends details with simplicity, and is capable of generating 4 different types of BaZi charts: **BaZi Professional Charts, BaZi Annual Analysis Charts, BaZi Pillar Analysis Charts and BaZi Family Relationship Charts.**

Joey Yap Feng Shui Template Set

Directions are the cornerstone of any successful Feng Shui audit or application. The **Joey Yap Feng Shui Template Set** is a set of three templates to simplify the process of taking directions and determining locations and positions, whether it's for a building, a house, or an open area such as a plot of land, all with just a floor plan or area map.

The Set comprises 3 basic templates: The Basic Feng Shui Template, 8 Mansions Feng Shui Template, and the Flying Stars Feng Shui Template.

Mini Feng Shui Compass

The Mini Feng Shui Compass is a self-aligning compass that is not only light at 100gms but also built sturdily to ensure it will be convenient to use anywhere. The rings on the Mini Feng Shui Compass are bi-lingual and incorporate the 24 Mountain Rings that is used in your traditional Luo Pan.

The comprehensive booklet included will guide you in applying the 24 Mountain Directions on your Mini Feng Shui Compass effectively and the 8 Mansions Feng Shui to locate the most auspicious locations within your home, office and surroundings. You can also use the Mini Feng Shui Compass when measuring the direction of your property for the purpose of applying Flying Stars Feng Shui.

www.masteryacademy.com | +603 - 2284 8080

Educational Tools and Software

Xuan Kong Vol.1
An Advanced Feng Shui Home Study Course

Learn the Xuan Kong Flying Star Feng Shui system in just 20 lessons! Joey Yap's specialised notes and course work have been written to enable distance learning without compromising on the breadth or quality of the syllabus. Learn at your own pace with the same material students in a live class would use. The most comprehensive distance learning course on Xuan Kong Flying Star Feng Shui in the market. Xuan Kong Flying Star Vol.1 comes complete with a special binder for all your course notes.

Feng Shui for Period 8 - (DVD)

Don't miss the Feng Shui Event of the next 20 years! Catch Joey Yap LIVE and find out just what Period 8 is all about. This DVD boxed set zips you through the fundamentals of Feng Shui and the impact of this important change in the Feng Shui calendar. Joey's entertaining, conversational style walks you through the key changes that Period 8 will bring and how to tap into Wealth Qi and Good Feng Shui for the next 20 years.

Xuan Kong Flying Stars Beginners Workshop - (DVD)

Take a front row seat in Joey Yap's Xuan Kong Flying Stars workshop with this unique LIVE RECORDING of Joey Yap's Xuan Kong Flying Stars Feng Shui workshop, attended by over 500 people. This DVD program provides an effective and quick introduction of Xuan Kong Feng Shui essentials for those who are just starting out in their study of classical Feng Shui. Learn to plot your own Flying Star chart in just 3 hours. Learn 'trade secret' methods, remedies and cures for Flying Stars Feng Shui. This boxed set contains 3 DVDs and 1 workbook with notes and charts for reference.

BaZi Four Pillars of Destiny Beginners Workshop - (DVD)

Ever wondered what Destiny has in store for you? Or curious to know how you can learn more about your personality and inner talents? BaZi or Four Pillars of Destiny is an ancient Chinese science that enables us to understand a person's hidden talent, inner potential, personality, health and wealth luck from just their birth data. This specially compiled DVD set of Joey Yap's BaZi Beginners Workshop provides a thorough and comprehensive introduction to BaZi. Learn how to read your own chart and understand your own luck cycle. This boxed set contains 3 DVDs and 1 workbook with notes and reference charts.

www.masteryacademy.com | +603 - 2284 8080

DVD Series

Joey Yap's Face Reading Revealed DVD Series

Mian Xiang, the Chinese art of Face Reading, is an ancient form of physiognomy and entails the use of the face and facial characteristics to evaluate key aspects of a person's life, luck and destiny. In his Face Reading DVDs series, Joey Yap shows you how the facial features reveal a wealth of information about a person's luck, destiny and personality.

Mian Xiang also tell us the talents, quirks and personality of an individual. Do you know that just by looking at a person's face, you can ascertain his or her health, wealth, relationships and career? Let Joey Yap show you how the 12 Palaces can be utilised to reveal a person's inner talents, characteristics and much more.

Feng Shui for Homebuyers DVD Series

In these DVDs, you will also learn how to identify properties with good Feng Shui features that will help you promote a fulfilling life and achieve your full potential. Discover how to avoid properties with negative Feng Shui that can bring about detrimental effects to your health, wealth and relationships.

Joey will also elaborate on how to fix the various aspects of your home that may have an impact on the Feng Shui of your property and give pointers on how to tap into the positive energies to support your goals.

Discover Feng Shui with Joey Yap: Set of 4 DVDs
Informative and entertaining, classical Feng Shui comes alive in *Discover Feng Shui with Joey Yap!*

You have the questions. Now let Joey personally answer them in this 4-set DVD compilation! Learn how to ensure the viability of your residence or workplace, Feng Shui-wise, without having to convert it into a Chinese antiques' shop. Classical Feng Shui is about harnessing the natural power of your environment to improve quality of life. It's a systematic and subtle metaphysical science.

Walking the Dragons with Joey Yap (The TV Series)

This DVD set features eight episodes, covering various landform Feng Shui analyses and applications from Joey Yap as he and his co-hosts travel through China. It includes case studies of both modern and historical sites with a focus on Yin House (burial places) Feng Shui and the tombs of the Qing Dynasty emperors.

The series was partly filmed on-location in mainland China, and the state of Selangor, Malaysia.

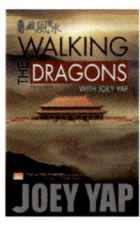

Home Study Courses

Gain Valuable Knowledge from the Comfort of Your Home

Now, armed with your trusty computer or laptop and Internet access, knowledge of Chinese Metaphysics is just a click away!

3 easy steps to activate your Home Study Course:

Step 1:
Go to the URL as indicated on the Activation Card, and key in your Activation Code

Step 2:
At the Registration page, fill in the details accordingly to enable us to generate your Student Identification (Student ID).

Step 3:
Upon successful registration, you may begin your lessons immediately.

Joey Yap's Feng Shui Mastery HomeStudy Course

Module 1: **Empowering Your Home**
Module 2: **Master Practitioner Program**

Learn how easy it is to harness the power of the environment to promote health, wealth and prosperity in your life. The knowledge and applications of Feng Shui will no more be a mystery but a valuable tool you can master on your own.

Joey Yap's BaZi Mastery HomeStudy Course

Module 1: **Mapping Your Life**
Module 2: **Mastering Your Future**

Discover your path of least resistance to success with insights about your personality and capabilities, and what strengths you can tap on to maximize your potential for success and happiness by mastering BaZi (Chinese Astrology). This course will teach you all the essentials you need to interpret a BaZi chart and more.

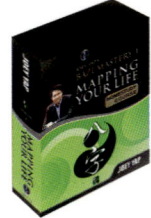 

Joey Yap's Mian Xiang Mastery HomeStudy Course

Module 1: **Face Reading**
Module 2: **Advanced Face Reading**

A face can reveal so much about a person. Now, you can learn the art and science of Mian Xiang (Chinese Face Reading) to understand a person's character based on his or her facial features with ease and confidence.

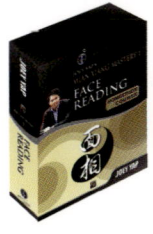 

www.masteryacademy.com | +603 - 2284 8080

Feng Shui Mastery™
LIVE COURSES (MODULES ONE TO FOUR)

The Feng Shui Mastery™ comprises Feng Shui Mastery Modules 1, 2, 3 and 4. It starts off with a foundation program up to the advanced practitioner level. It is a thorough, comprehensive program that covers important theories from various classical Feng Shui systems including Ba Zhai, San Yuan, San He, and Xuan Kong.

Module One: Beginners Course   **Module Two:** Practitioners Course   **Module Three:** Advanced Practitioners Course   **Module Four:** Master Course

BaZi Mastery™
LIVE COURSES (MODULES ONE TO FOUR)

The BaZi Mastery™ consists of BaZi Mastery Modules 1, 2, 3 and 4. In Modules 1 and 2, students will receive a thorough introduction to BaZi, along with an intensive understanding of BaZi principles and the requisite skills to practice it with accuracy and precision. This will prepare them, and serious Feng Shui practitioners, for a more advanced levels and fine-tune their application skills in Modules 3 and 4.

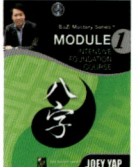   

Module One: Intensive Foundation Course   **Module Two:** Practitioners Course   **Module Three:** Advanced Practitioners Course   **Module Four:** Master Course in BaZi

# Xuan Kong Mastery™
LIVE COURSES (MODULES ONE TO THREE)
* Advanced Courses For Master Practitioners

The Xuan Kong Mastery™ comprises Xuan Kong Mastery Modules 1, 2A, 2B and 3. It is a sophisticated branch of Feng Shui replete with many techniques and formulae, enabling practitioners to evaluate Feng Shui on a more thorough and in-depth basis. The study of Xuan Kong encompasses numerology, symbology and science of the Ba Gua along with the mathematics of time.

 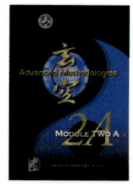 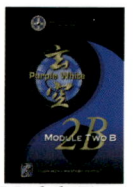 

Module One: Advanced Foundation Course   **Module Two A:** Advanced Xuan Kong Methodologies   **Module Two B:** Purple White   **Module Three:** Advanced Xuan Kong Da Gua

www.masteryacademy.com | +603 - 2284 8080

Mian Xiang Mastery™
LIVE COURSES (MODULES ONE AND TWO)

The Mian Xiang Mastery™ comprises of Mian Xiang Mastery Modules 1 and 2 to allow students to learn this ancient art in a thorough, detailed manner. Each module has a carefully-developed syllabus that allows students to get acquainted with the fundamentals of Mian Xiang before moving on to the more intricate theories and principles that will enable them to practice Mian Xiang with greater depth and complexity.

Module One:
Basic Face Reading

Module Two:
Practical Face Reading

Yi Jing Mastery™
LIVE COURSES (MODULES ONE AND TWO)

The Yi Jing Mastery™ comprises Modules 1 and 2. Both Modules aim to give casual and serious Yi Jing enthusiasts a serious insight into one of the most important philosophical treatises in ancient Chinese thought. Yi Jing uses sophisticated formulas and calculations to derive the answers to questions we pose. It is a science of divination, and in our classes there is a heavy emphasis on the scientific aspect of it. It bears no religious or superstitious affiliation.

Module One:
Traditional Yi Jing

Module Two:
Plum Blossom Numerology

Ze Ri Mastery™
LIVE COURSES (MODULES ONE AND TWO)

The ZeRi Mastery™ consists of ZeRi Mastery Modules 1 and 2. This program provides students with a thorough introduction to the art of Date Selection both for Personal and Feng Shui purposes. Our ZeRi Mastery™ aims to provide a thorough and comprehensive program on the art of Date Selection, covering everything from Personal and Feng Shui Date Selection to Xuan Kong Da Gua Date Selection.

Module One:
Personal and Feng Shui Date Selection

Module Two:
Xuan Kong Da Gua Date Selection

www.masteryacademy.com | +603 - 2284 8080

Feng Shui for Life

This is an entry-level five-day course designed for the Feng Shui beginner to learn the application of practical Feng Shui in day-to-day living. Lessons include quick tips on analyzing the BaZi chart, simple Feng Shui solutions for the home, basic Date Selection, useful Face Reading techniques and practical Water formulas. A great introduction course on Chinese Metaphysics studies for beginners.

Joey Yap's
Design Your Destiny

This is a three-day life transformation program designed to inspire awareness and action for you to create a better quality of life. It introduces the DRT™ (Decision Referential Technology) method, which utilizes the BaZi Personality Profiling system to determine the right version of you, and serves as a tool to help you make better decisions and achieve a better life in the least resistant way possible based on your Personality Profile Type.

Walk the Mountains! Learn Feng Shui in a Practical and Hands-on Program

 ### Feng Shui Mastery Excursion™

Learn landform (Luan Tou) Feng Shui by walking the mountains and chasing the Dragon's vein in China. This Program takes the students in a study tour to examine notable Feng Shui landmarks, mountains, hills, valleys, ancient palaces, famous mansions, houses and tombs in China. The Excursion is a 'practical' hands-on course where students are shown to perform readings using the formulas they've learnt and to recognize and read Feng Shui Landform (Luan Tou) formations.

Read about China Excursion here:
http://www.fengshuiexcursion.com

Mastery Academy courses are conducted around the world. Find out when will Joey Yap be in your area by visiting **www.masteryacademy.com** or call our office at **+603-2284 8080**.